# Journey

# Alec Motyer

# Journey

## Psalms for pilgrim people

ivp

INTER-VARSITY PRESS
Norton Street, Nottingham NG7 3HR, England
*Email: ivp@ivpbooks.com*
*Website: www.ivpbooks.com*

*First published 2009*

**British Library Cataloguing in Publication Data**
A catalogue record for this book is available from the British Library.

ISBN: 978-1-84474-355-1

Set in 10.5/13pt Dante
Typeset in Great Britain by CRB Associates, Reepham, Norfolk
Printed and bound in Great Britain by Cromwell Press, Trowbridge

Inter-Varsity Press publishes Christian books that are true to the Bible and that communicate the gospel, develop discipleship and strengthen the church for its mission in the world.

Inter-Varsity Press is closely linked with the Universities and Colleges Christian Fellowship, a student movement connecting Christian Unions in universities and colleges throughout Great Britain, and a member movement of the International Fellowship of Evangelical Students. Website: *www.uccf.org.uk*

To
my dearest fellow pilgrim,
my wife, Beryl,
to commemorate our Diamond Wedding,
30 August 2008,
with love and gratitude

# Contents

## Abbreviations

| AV | Authorized or King James Version of 1611 |
| BDB | Brown-Driver-Briggs Hebrew–English Lexicon |
| ESV | English Standard Version (2001) |
| JerB | Jerusalem Bible |
| NASB | New American Standard Bible (1960) |
| NKJV | New King James Version or RAV Revised Authorized Version (1982) |
| NRSV | New Revised Standard Version (1989) |
| RSV | Revised Standard Version (1946, 1952) |
| RV | Revised Version of 1880 |
| √ | Root form of the Hebrew verb in question |
| < > | References are added in angled brackets where chapter and/or verse numbers in the Hebrew Bible are different from English versions |

# Preface

These studies of the 'Songs of the Great Ascent' had their one and only public airing at the Weston-super-Mare Christian Convention in July 1978. Since then much water has flowed under the bridge – in terms of additional commentaries studied, and further work done, especially for the entry on Psalms in the *New Bible Commentary, 21st Century Edition*, (IVP, 1994). More recently my son, Stephen, said – with an element of surprise? – 'Your idea that the Songs of Ascent are in triads really works!' He then went on to suggest writing the whole series up in fuller form. What could I do but obey?

The observation about triadic arrangement is not, however, original with me. I picked up the clue in W. E. Barnes' *Westminster Commentary on Psalms* (Methuen, 1931), though Barnes did not, as a matter of fact, develop the suggestion.

As ever I am deeply in the debt of the Inter-Varsity Press for accepting my work for publication, and in particular to Mrs Kate Byrom, the commissioning editor, and, behind her, unnamed 'hands' who have read the manuscript and helped me so much. I am very grateful. To be cared for by the Press and its officers is a very special privilege.

What Psalm 127 says about house-building and urban security is just as true about book-writing. 'All we can do is nothing worth except God blesses the deed.' May he therefore be pleased to take this book and use it not only to throw light on Psalms 120 – 136 but also to lead every reader into a deeper love of the word of God and a fuller commitment to its truth.

And finally. Rightly this book is dedicated to Beryl, but she would heartily join me in praise to the Lord who has (so far) allowed us sixty years of the deepest happiness, an act of his sheer grace to which we respond in glad and grateful worship.

Alec Motyer
Poynton, Cheshire
2009

# 1  Are you going up this year?

So often, the simplest way to understand something is the best.

What is possibly the loveliest single group of psalms in the whole collection, Psalms 120 – 134 describe themselves as 'Songs of Ascents'. Like all the titles of individual psalms, this is to be taken seriously as a pointer to how the psalm in question is to be understood and used. The plural word 'ascents' could be what in Hebrew is called a 'plural of magnitude' – 'the Great Ascent', or it can be left as a simple plural, an 'ascent' that happened over and over again. Either way, it readily points to the journeys of pilgrims from all over the land 'up' to Jerusalem to keep the Feasts of the Lord.

This is the most direct interpretation of the title, and far less fanciful than some other suggestions that have been made. It also happens to be one that suits the psalms themselves very well, and, as we shall see, also suits the way in which they have been carefully edited into this small collection. In order to keep this in mind we will generally use the translation 'Songs of the Ascent' or 'of the Great Ascent'.

## Walking, running and arriving

But we must not get ahead of ourselves! Surprisingly, neither the verbs 'to go on a pilgrimage' and 'to be a pilgrim' nor the nouns 'pilgrim' and 'pilgrimage' appear in the Bible! There are five places where some translations[1] introduce the thought, but, as far as the Hebrew of the Old Testament and the Greek of the New are concerned, they do so without justification. In Genesis 47:9, Exodus 6:4 and Psalm 119:54 the word means 'sojourning', being a temporary resident or even an overnight guest,[2] and in Hebrews 11:13 and 1 Peter 2:11 we need a translation like 'resident alien' or, perhaps, 'expatriate'.[3]

The words of pilgrimage, then, are not used, but the pilgrim idea is deeply ingrained right through the Bible, and not only in the official sense in which what we would call pilgrimages to Jerusalem were commanded once our ancestors were settled in the Promised Land, but on the level of individual devotion. Can we avoid saying that the Lord called Abram 'to be a pilgrim'? Hebrews 11:8 could not be clearer: Abraham was called to leave Ur of the Chaldees and he obeyed even though 'he did not know where he was going' – a pilgrim indeed! Reaching Canaan and learning that this was the land of promise (Genesis 17:7) did not change anything, but simply redefined Abraham's role, for his calling was still to 'walk before me' (Genesis 17:1).

Presently, in connection with the psalms of the Great Ascent, we will call this 'the pilgrimage of the heart', our daily 'walking with God'. It is in this way, indeed, that 'pilgrimage' becomes a central Bible truth. Think, for example, of the fact that, early on, Christianity was called 'the way';[4] that is to say, not only a set of beliefs, nor only an unforgettable experience of accepting the Lord Jesus Christ as our own personal Saviour, but a pathway for life, a distinctive lifestyle, truth to be lived out, ideals to be pursued, goals to be set and striven for. Above all, a perfect Jesus to be imitated, for all these references find their root in his claim that 'I am the way' (John 14:6).

It is more than a bit sad that the NIV has chosen to obscure the matching metaphor of 'walking'. After all, we say to new parents, 'Is the baby walking yet?' 'Walking' is one of the earliest and most prized signs of a properly developing life, and it is no wonder that the New Testament makes full use of it in relation to Christian living. Ephesians almost hammers us with our vocation to 'walk worthily of our calling'

(Ephesians 4:1), to 'walk no longer as the Gentiles also walk' (4:17), to 'walk in love' (5:1), to 'walk as children of light' (5:8), and to 'look carefully how we walk, not as unwise but as wise' (5:15);[5] walking is, you see, a pretty comprehensive description of the Christian's progress as a growing entity from infancy to adulthood, with proper, balanced development, inwardly and outwardly: a pilgrimage of conduct, character, mind and heart. We will find that the psalms of the Great Ascent speak to us of all this, in their own distinctive and uniformly lovely way.

Have you noticed the 'golden cord' that binds Hebrews 10, 11 and 12? Hebrews 10:39 says that 'we are those who believe and are saved'. More literally, we are 'of faith'. That is our hallmark – faith. Hebrews 11:1 starts, 'now faith is . . . ', because if faith is our central characteristic, we need to know what we are talking about. This is the point of the marvellous picture gallery of Hebrews 11: faith as seen in the lives of such a varied and instructive band. And so into Hebrews 12 where the initial 'therefore' alerts us to what is about to happen. The people of faith surround us like a cloud, and their testimony to what faith is, how it works, and so on, summons us to 'run with perseverance the race marked out for us' with our eyes fixed on Jesus. The life of faith is on the run! Pilgrims on the run! I hope I am right in seeing this, not as a picture of speed – for many of us, days of speed are long gone – but of urgency, of the need to be up and doing, so that even when the feet are unfit for the sandals of the pilgrim walk, never mind the running shoes of the athletic track, the pilgrimage of the heart is our daily preoccupation, and to fix our eyes on Jesus our moment-by-moment preoccupation.

But, before we return to the psalms, we must take a brief moment to look forward to the pilgrims' goal. Some glad day, for us, as for the pilgrims on the great ascent, travelling days will be over and our mobile home will be exchanged for a house, but one not made with hands, eternal in the heavens (2 Corinthians 5:1), and, in the dramatic words of Revelation 22:14 (NKJV), we will 'enter through the gates into the city'. An elderly couple, treasured friends of mine, once qualified for tickets to one of the Queen's garden parties. As they parked their car, a well-meaning policeman came up and, pointing to a small door, said, 'If you like to go through there you will find yourselves in the garden and save yourselves a long walk.' They drew themselves up to their full height, and replied: 'We have been invited by Her Majesty. Do you really think we are going in through a back gate?'

What a day it will be when the gates swing wide, the trumpets sound, and all the bells of the heavenly city ring out in delirious celebration!

> From earth's wide bounds, from ocean's furthest coast,
> Through gates of pearl stream in the countless host,
> Singing to Father, Son and Holy Ghost,
> Hallelujah[6]

That's what walking the pilgrim way is 'all about'. But we must get back to the psalms.

### Never forget your salvation

Three pilgrimages were ordered every year. What an undertaking! Old Testament religion was hugely exuberant, given to singing and all sorts of vocal, physical and instrumental participation,[7] but it was far from undemanding. Think of the expense of providing animals for the required sacrifices; think of time out from farm, shop or home; think of protracted journeys, with all the attendant hazards of bodily effort, never mind possible attack by brigands. All that – but also read these wonderful psalms and hear them singing as they go up. They were pilgrims on a demanding pilgrimage, but pilgrims with a song in their heart and on their lips, paying the price of their pilgrimage with gladness, joyful to walk with their God, and to make their way home to his house.

### Why?

It is, however, very important indeed to understand why they went and why they sang. Such a costly effort might seem to suggest trying by good works to earn 'brownie points' with God – earning our own salvation. But when we read what the Old Testament actually says about the pilgrim feasts we find that such an interpretation is ruled out. In

Exodus 23:14–17, the first required pilgrim feast was Passover (compare Exodus 12), the annual remembrance of the lamb slain in Egypt so that the Lord's people could shelter under its blood. As they sheltered they were both kept safe (12:13, 22–23) and made into the Lord's pilgrim people (12:11). The lamb that died in Egypt was a once-for-all divine provision of salvation; the annual Passover sacrifice could only go on remembering something that could never, in fact, be repeated – and that 'something' was no act or effort or provision we made, but the Lord's work of grace, his appointed way of salvation.[8]

The second pilgrim feast ordered in Exodus was Harvest, and the third 'Ingathering', or 'Tabernacles'. When we read what is said elsewhere about these two feasts,[9] we learn that each one of them was also, in its own way, a remembrance of servitude in Egypt and of divine deliverance. In other words, all three pilgrim feasts were extended, annual opportunities to recall what the Lord had provided and done for the salvation of his people, what they were saved from, and how their salvation was a divine provision of power and effectiveness of which they were the beneficiaries, but to which they made no contribution.

## Effective remembrance

To be frank, it all makes our Christmas and Easter festivities seem pretty episodic and perfunctory. For one day we recall 'the wondrous cross on which the Prince of glory died'; for one day we celebrate his birth – with family merrymaking – and his resurrection – with a Sunday-morning service. By comparison, the Lord extended Passover into the week-long Feast of Unleavened Bread[10] – the use of unleavened bread being (whatever else) a demand for simplicity of lifestyle in order that time might be given to living in the afterglow of Passover. Add to this the time taken walking to Jerusalem and returning home! How important in the Lord's estimation it is that his people should take time out to live thoughtfully, consciously and with commitment in the light of what he has done for them: his work of salvation.

Maybe, then, there is more than a hint that we should pay more attention to 'the twelve days of Christmas', for example, as the proper period of remembrance – though, please, no one send me six lords a-leaping, or whatever! Indeed, to take another example, it is not all that long ago that the week before Easter was widely respected as 'Holy Week', with each day in some measure used to help us to follow Jesus from his entry to Jerusalem to his last supper (which was also, of course, the *first* Lord's Supper), then to his substitutionary death, on to the solemnity of his entombment, and finally 'to see upon the shining skies, the Sun of Righteousness arise, on that first Easter morn'.[11]

## So it was commanded . . . so it was done!

For another experience of sun rising, try reading straight out of the Book of Judges into Ruth and Samuel as a continuous narrative. Judges is an almost unrelieved story of failure and, finally, corruption. At the top end of society, the 'judges', with their glittering deeds, failed to bring any lasting solution to national ills,[12] and underneath, at grass-roots level, life was festering in every department.[13] What a relief to enter the Book of Ruth,[14] where the Lord dominates the whole story; people speak of him, and greet each other in his name (Ruth 2:4–5). In other words, alongside the darkness of the Judges record, there is more to be told. There was still a wholesomeness in life and society; religious decline on the one hand was matched by religious devotion on the other.

And this is equally the case when we read on into 1 Samuel. We meet the bluff and godly (even if somewhat insensitive – 1:8) Elkanah, well out of his depth with his two womenfolk, yet taking the lead in family religious life, and taking them on pilgrimage to Shiloh. It is a sharply drawn picture of Old Testament religion in action – its devotedness, seriousness and spirituality – but, for our purposes, it reveals the keeping of pilgrimage. People did honour their obligation of appearing before the Lord in the place he chose – even if Elkanah may have limited himself to once a year (1 Samuel 1:21).[15]

Interestingly, at the start of the New Testament, we find the same practice being followed, and we accompany the wonderful Joseph and Mary as they make their annual Passover trip to Jerusalem (Luke 2:41), and as, when the time came, they bring the twelve-year-old Jesus with them.

### And as they went, they sang

The 'Songs of the Ascent' give us a window into one aspect of the pilgrim journey. Luke 2:44 shows that the pilgrims travelled in large groups in which 'relatives and friends' made the journey together. It would be nice to know more, but it is not overstretching the imagination to think of each pilgrimage day beginning and ending in worship and song. Nor is it too much to suppose that, in Jerusalem, different groups spoke together about the hymns they had enjoyed en route, and that over the course of the years someone collected and edited 'old favourites' into a hymn book, which became widely used – and, maybe, called 'Pilgrim Praise'. Who can tell? Equally, who can deny?

What is clear is that such a group of pilgrimage psalms was finally incorporated, just as it stood, into the larger collection of the Songs of Israel, which we call the Book of Psalms.

In the Old Testament, 'singing' is a 'motif' for entering with joy into what the Lord has done for us (compare Exodus 15:1; Psalm 98:1). It is the way we express our glad appreciation of the God who saves and of a salvation to which we contribute nothing, for our joy is responsive not contributory. Pilgrim praise is now part of the imperishable word of God; the Lord's people are still his pilgrims, singing as we journey, not to an earthly Zion but to that heavenly Zion to which we already belong (Hebrews 12:22), and to which we aim as our eternal home (Revelation 21:9–10, 27).

---

### Notes

1 E.g. AV, NKJV.
2 The verbal forms and the nouns all derive from √*gur*, to sojourn, stay a while.
3 Greek *parepidymos*.
4 Acts 9:2; 19:9, 23; 22:4; 24:14; 2 Peter 2:2.
5 Quoted from the Revised Version.
6 W. W. How, 'For all the saints who from their labours rest'.
7 Use the Book of Psalms as a window into Old Testament life and worship. There was singing, clapping and shouting (e.g. 47:1, 5, 7), full involvement of every personal and instrumental source of praise

(Psalm 150), processions (42:4) and gestures (63:4) – as well, of course, as meditative rest before God (62:1, 5).

8 On Passover, see Alec Motyer, *The Message of Exodus* (IVP, 2006), pp. 131–137, etc; *Discovering the Old Testament* (IVP, 2006), pp. 79–82.

9 E.g. Deuteronomy 26:1–11; Leviticus 23:39–43.

10 Exodus 12:17–20.

11 Timothy Dudley-Smith's hymn 'By loving hands the Lord is laid'. For the full text, *A house of praise*, 157, (OUP, 2003).

12 Judges 1 – 16. The recurring refrain of the judges is that they gave the land rest for a limited period, after which things returned to what they were before (e.g. 3:11; 8:28).

13 Judges 17 – 21 reveal corruption in religion (17:1–13), society (18:1–31), morality (19:1–30) and national unity (20:1 – 21:25). The stories are so vividly told that the reader can almost smell the rottenness!

14 In the Hebrew Bible Ruth is found among 'the Writings', the third and last section in the collection. Samuel follows Judges directly. English Bibles accept the order of books in the Greek translation, the Septuagint.

15 The Bible does not say that Elkanah's annual trip was at a festival time – Passover or otherwise. It seems reasonable to assume that it was, but in any case it records the practice of pilgrimage.

## 2  The pilgrims' songbook

The psalms officially described as 'Songs of the Ascent' start at Psalm 120 and end with Psalm 134. I have ventured to include Psalms 135 and 136 as a grand, concluding, shout of praise. The singing pilgrims keep singing even when they reach their destination!

The Songs of the Ascent form a collection notable for beauty of thought and expression; it is also notable for careful, indeed clever, editing.[1]

### A revealing bracket

Right through the Psalms – and even in prose works as well as poetry outside the Psalms – it is worth training ourselves as readers to look out for a literary feature called 'inclusio', or 'inclusion'. This is when writers round off a section by returning to the point at which they started. Usually this means saying the same thing (though not, of course, necessarily in the same words), or making the same sort of allusion, always with amplification or development, and sometimes with sharp contrast. The effect is to create a 'bracket', announcing the rounding-off of maybe a section within a longer poem, or of the poem itself, or, in the case of the Songs of the Ascent, of the whole group.

Seemingly strangely, but actually very tellingly, the bracket round the Songs of the Ascent is 'darkness'.

In Psalm 120 the writer positions himself in Kedar (verse 5). We will discuss presently where this was and in what sense he came to be there, but, as a word, 'Kedar' comes from a verb meaning 'to be black, dark' (e.g. Jeremiah 4:28), and the place may have acquired its name from the black tents of its nomadic inhabitants. The location is well chosen. He lives in 'darkness' and many factors block the sunlight out of his life: 'distress' (verse 1), untruthfulness (verse 2), surrounding inveterate hostility (verses 6–7). Pilgrimage out of such a place would come as a welcome relief. Imagine leaving that 'Kedar' for the company of those who were walking with God, singing his songs, and heading for his city, house and presence![2]

But when they arrive (Psalm 134), it is to experience still more darkness. Yet how blessedly different! They stand by night in the house of the Lord. On their part they urge the officiants of the house to lift their hands in worship and their voices in praise; in return the voice of benediction calls on 'the LORD, the Maker of heaven and earth' to bless his pilgrims, now, at last, arrived and safely enclosed in his presence. The hostility of darkness has been replaced by the gentle 'blanket' of the overshadowing night sky; the voices of untruth and hostility by the voices of praise and blessing; Kedar by Zion.

### Mini-pilgrimages

Careful editing of the Songs of the Ascent goes beyond where they begin and where they end. Internally, the collection (Psalms 120 – 134) is set out in five groups of three psalms each, and each group – apart from the last – consists of what we might call a mini-pilgrimage.

The first psalm in each group of three (120, 123, 126 and 129) describes a situation of stress and distress. Look at a key verse in each:

** 120:5: Isolated in an uncongenial world
** 123:4: When endurance seems at an end

** 126:2, 5: Laughter belongs in the past, tears in the present
** 129:5: Despite past defeats, Zion's enemies remain

The second psalm in each group of three (121, 124, 127 and 130) focuses on the Lord's power to save, deliver, build and strengthen, and to keep hope alive:

** 121:2: Help comes from the Lord
** 124:1: The Lord is on our side
** 127:1, 2: The Lord builds up and gives sweet rest
** 130:7, 8: Not even sin can prevail against the Lord

In summary, the leading psalm in each triad recalls the trials, discomforts and threats of life in this world; the second psalm points to an all-sufficient God. The third psalm in each case brings us home: we are at last 'in harbour'; we have arrived; Zion's citizens safe in Zion.

** 122:2: 'Our feet are standing in your gates, O Jerusalem'
** 125:1: Zion cannot be shaken; nor can we
** 128: Blessed in work (2), in home (3), and in Zion (5)
** 131:2: Sheer contentment

**Two pilgrimages; one homecoming**

Two things remain to be noticed about the editorial scheme of the Songs of the Ascent.

First, when we come to Psalms 126 – 131, the third and fourth triads, there is a change of emphasis. Suddenly the theme is no longer, so to speak, the dangers of the road, circumstantial threats to pilgrimage in one way and another, but rather longing for the Lord's blessing. Thus Psalm 126 longs for a fresh experience of blessing such as used to be enjoyed; 127 and 128 look for his prospering in city, home and family; 130 faces up to sin and alienation from God, and 131 brings the pilgrim to rest with the Lord as a toddler with his or her mother. In other words, our pilgrimage is a twin-track affair. On the one hand we are making our way forward to Zion through an alien and hostile world; on the other hand, we are making progress in our walk with God, a pilgrimage of the heart and of personal devotion.

In the final triad, Psalms 132 – 134, both of these 'pilgrimages' reach their destination. As a group they are Zion-centred psalms. We are no longer – as the old hymn used to say – 'marching upward to Zion, the beautiful city of God';[3] we have arrived: David secured the specialness of Zion by finding and placing the Ark of the Lord there, and making it the seat of his dynasty (132);[4] 'brothers' come there into a glorious unity, and experience the blessing of life that such unity alone brings (133), and from the house of the Lord blessing is pronounced on his worshippers, keeping vigil (134). Safe in Zion indeed – and at home with God!

You will find it helpful to read through the psalms along with the following chart. You might like even to cheat a bit by sneaking a look at chapters 9 and 16.

| Psalms 120 – 125 The pilgrim path facing life | The uncongenial world | Our sufficient God | Home in Zion |
|---|---|---|---|
| | 120 (hostility) | 121 (keeping) | 122 (joy) |
| | 123 (contempt) | 124 (competent) | 125 (security) |
| Psalms 126 – 131 Walking with God A pilgrimage of the heart | Sorrows and trials | Our reliable God | Blessing and peace in Zion |
| | 126 (patience) | 127 (rest) | 128 (blessing now and to come) |
| | 129 (trusting in trials) | 130 (mercy) | 131 (a calm companionship) |
| Psalms 132 – 134 The assured glory | 132 The city of the king | 133 Its people, united and blessed | 134 Peace and worship We with Him; He with us |

## Notes

1 The same is true of other collections incorporated into the Book of Psalms. See 'Royal Praise' (Psalms 93 – 100), 'Salvation Praise' (Psalms 113 – 118) and 'Endless Praise' (Psalms 146 – 150). Alec Motyer, 'The Psalms' in *New Bible Commentary: 21st Century Edition* (IVP, 1994). The triadic arrangement of the Songs of Ascent was noticed by W. E. Barnes, *The Psalms, Westminster Commentary*, 2 vols. (Methuen, 1931).

2 Compare Psalm 43:2–4: out of mourning into the light; coming ever nearer; first the place, then the altar, finally 'to God, my joy and my delight'.

3 The hymn 'Come, ye that love the Lord' in the version by H. A. C. Malan, *Sacred Songs and Solos*, 823; *Hymns of Faith*, 363.

4 2 Samuel 5:6–9; 6:1–17.

Psalm 120

## 3 The resident alien: Living in the unwelcome present

That title just about sums up Psalm 120.

In Dublin, in the 1930s, there was a pretty special man called T. C. Hammond. Unfortunately for us, he emigrated to Australia. Not only was he a person of truly awesome learning, but he was also more than something of a 'character'. At the time of a general election, someone posed the question; 'Mr Hammond, we are citizens of heaven, not of earth, so how can we vote in a general election?' 'Well, Madam,' replied Hammond, 'it's like this: if you can't vote as a citizen, why don't you vote as a lodger?'

How true! We are caught between the upper and the lower millstones of a heavenly and an earthly citizenship. The former will be all bliss, once we get there; the latter is a mixed blessing, and, sometimes, our sense of being out of kilter with our surroundings becomes just too much to bear. Of course, that word 'sometimes' is important. The wise book of Ecclesiastes rightly urges us to grasp life's enrichments and enjoyments with both hands, and live it to the full (Ecclesiastes 5:18–19), for the earth is still the Lord's (Psalms 24:1). Yet time and again we see and feel those other realities that drive home our alienation, and provoke in us a sweet homesickness. We are tied up at an alien quayside, waiting for the Pilot to take us out to sea and back to our home port.

## The believer: an ethnic minority

It is just such a moment that Psalm 120 captures. The psalmist is not quite at the end of his tether, but the constant sense of alienation, the ceaseless strife of tongues, is eroding his will to live. The lies and deceit that are his portion (verses 1–2) are so incessant that it seems to him as if a war has been declared (verses 6–7). He just can't settle comfortably in this world. His unease is actually caused by sins of speech, but the reason for his discomfort is a basic, irreconcilable tension between himself and his contemporaries.

These are the matters that we must sort out in a little more detail.

### The world

The writer of Psalm 120 looked round him and came to the conclusion, 'I just don't belong' – and he was right! John's Gospel puts it like this: 'He (Jesus, the Word) was in the world . . . the world did not recognize him' (John 1:10). 'The world' is a whole scheme of things, a way of life, a philosophy or set of ideas, a man-made system that has no room for Jesus, no understanding of who he is, no opening of the door to receive him. This is 'the world' as Jesus found it: a place of hatred in which, as he warned his disciples, they too must be ready to face hatred. They do not belong any more than he[1] (John 15:18, 19). According to the psalmist, this was equally true of old. His world was a place of 'distress' (1), or 'adversity', not trouble arising by accident but of trouble caused by an opposition and animosity inherent in the scheme of things and in the people who belong to it. He needed deliverance (2) as from dangerous foes. The sheer discomfort of his situation caused him to give vent to what one writer has called 'a deep, heaving sigh' (verse 5),[2] to which verse 6 adds that he has had just about enough of contemporaries who are as diametrically opposed to him as war is to peace (7).

### The tongue

Now prepare to be surprised. We know that life is just like that for some people, and that there was no element of exaggeration in anything the psalmist said. But would we have guessed in advance precisely where the hostility between church and world showed itself? The tongue and speech! We might have proposed ten or twelve other things, and never once put our finger on the tongue as the main characteristic of 'the world'. Yet there it is. He consulted his circumstances, asked himself why he felt so ill at ease and sought to pinpoint the cause of his discomfort, and the answer was the characteristic speech of his peers.

** verse 2a: 'lying lips', literally, 'a lip of falsehood'. You have heard, perhaps, the jibe made against some (usually prominent) person: 'But if you see his lips move you know he is telling a lie.' This caricature was all too true for the psalmist. 'A lip of falsehood' is one in which falsehood lives; lip and lie have become one entity.

** verse 2b, 'deceitful tongues', is, in the Hebrew, two nouns in apposition, a construction used to assert that the one is in truth the same as the other, and vice versa. We could put an equals sign between them – literally 'a tongue that is deceit itself':

** verse 7: the tongue at war. Talk was the point at which the dislocation between the psalmist and the society he lived in became, on their part, open warfare. 'I am a man of peace' is a reasonable rendering of words that cannot be set down literally. 'I am peace' is the writer's claim: two nouns in apposition, matching, in the balanced structure of the psalm, 'a tongue that is deceit' in verse 2. Would we catch the force of the words with 'peace is my middle name'? He has identified himself with peace, and peace has been 'made flesh' in him. 'Peace' – personal, social and spiritual wholeness and well-being – is what he is 'all about', his whole demeanour, his innermost desire and purpose, his thoughts and relationships; but as soon as he opens his mouth – not just to 'speak peace' but whatever he says – World War 3 breaks out!

### Judgment to come

Of course, it is not really what we think that matters, but what God thinks, and the judgment to come – or, if you like, the end of the world – is the final, unmistakeable revelation of his mind, the moment when he enforces and stands by what he values. So, regarding the importance or unimportance of sins of speech, our sadly relative and unreliable sense of values might reply, 'So what?', but what does God say? The answer comes in verses 3–4.

The NIV is to be preferred in translating the (Hebrew) third person singular verbs in verse 3 as referring to divine action.[3] The psalm brings the issue of the 'lip of falsehood' and the 'tongue which is deceit itself' before the bar of the coming Judge, and is in no doubt about the verdict.

Then, the war-makers of verse 7 will find that not only has war been declared on them, but the battle has been won and is all over.

** 'Arrows' are a weapon of combat from a distance. 'Warrior' implies skill and accuracy – the arrows as of a trained bowman. There is no flight from such (e.g. 2 Kings 9:23, 24). The arrow is a weapon not of mass destruction, but of individual fatality. The Lord's justice falls exactly where it is deserved.

** 'burning coals'[4] alludes poetically to the gathering and burning of the detritus of battle after the victory has been won (e.g. Isaiah 9:5). But, of course, as ever, fire symbolizes the active holiness of the Lord in its hostility to all sin. Compare Isaiah 6:3–6.

** 'More besides' does not mean that the Lord in judgment 'goes over the top', imposing a more severe punishment than the offence merits, but that he fully apportions the sentence his absolute justice has passed.

## So . . . ?

We too live in 'the world', and, for so many of us, it is a congenial place. We readily fit in with its prevailing lifestyle, and, often to an astonishing degree, accept current norms of behaviour. A candid onlooker might find it difficult to point to any serious difference between believer and unbeliever outside Sunday morning. Those of us, however, who recall now-distant 'earlier days' cannot but smile at the prohibitions forced on us by our 'elders and betters' who were earnestly intent on keeping us from the insidious ways of 'the world'. Looking back, indeed, so much of it was silly: hurtfully restrictive to the Christian without being impressive to the onlooker. So, out has gone the baby with the bath water! The old lines of demarcation between the church and the world were no longer meaningful, so the lines were erased, and, as someone once put it to me, it was like Robinson Crusoe who, in kindness, made the enclosure for his goats so spacious that the goats inside were as wild as the goats outside!

But the point is a serious one, is it not? We are, after all, called to be the Lord's distinct, readily identifiable people. Think how the law of the Lord through Moses called his people, for example, to eat a different diet from others by distinguishing 'clean' and 'unclean food' (Deuteronomy 14), not arbitrarily but because they were holy, separated to the Lord, and his precious treasure (Deuteronomy 14:2); they were to show their distinctiveness even in the way they dressed (Deuteronomy 22:11), in their sexual rules (Leviticus 18); indeed, over the whole of their life before the watching world, by the revealed word that they obeyed (Deuteronomy 4:6), they were called to excite the world's admiration. But, by comparison, we have to admit that there is little about us that marks us out, or that makes us sigh deeply that 'we dwell in Meshech . . . among the tents of Kedar' (verse 5).

'Meshech' was away to the remote north of Israel; Kedar was an Ishmaelite tribe of the northern Arabian desert.[5] No one could be geographically in both places at once – not actually, only spiritually! This is the point: he could not have *felt* more alienated from his surroundings if he were exiled far away, living among the uncircumcised – those to whom the promises of the Lord had never been made or sealed, witness to savage inhumanities and under divine judgment.

So, yes, let us chuckle and regret the artificial 'separations' encouraged in the past, but let us beware of settling cosily into our world and neglecting the duty of a distinct and distinctive life. If there is no element of 'deep sighing' – not 'tut-tutting' or head-shaking in mock sorrow, but the deep sigh of unsettlement and longing for home – then it's high time to wake up, put on the armour of light again, and dress ourselves with the Lord Jesus Christ as the national garb of our homeland (Romans 13:11–14). 'For we will all stand before God's judgment seat' (Romans 14:10; 2 Corinthians 5:10).

In particular, urges Psalm 120, guard against and fly from misuse of the tongue. The tongue has such a capacity to hurt and destroy that James – doing no more than taking the same attitude as prevails throughout the Bible – could speak of it as a fire, causing conflagration, and itself ignited in hell (James 3:5, 6). Remember how Isaiah found himself banished and doomed – along with his people – because of 'unclean lips' (6:5). Maybe in this more than in anything else we find it easy to overlook the fact that 'what is highly valued among men is detestable in God's sight' (Luke 16:15), but Jesus said so, and the same applies to things humans treat as of no consequence. Jesus also said that every 'careless word' will be brought into judgment, and that our words hold the balance between condemnation and acquittal (Matthew 12:36, 37). No wonder, then, that 'if anyone is never at fault in what he says, he is a perfect man' (James 3:2).

## Praying in a difficult day

Psalm 120 is a poem in three parts:

A[1] Answered prayer (vv. 1–2): Problem solved?
It is never an easy matter to translate the Hebrew verbal tenses. The two verbs in verse 1 are what is called 'perfect tense', but is it here a past tense – looking back to a particular moment when prayer was made and at once answered (the NKJV understands it like this)? Or is it, as in the NIV, a perfect verb expressing invariable experience – prayer made, prayer answered? Either way – but, I think, with preference for a past tense here, prayer and answer go together.

B Coming judgment (vv. 3–4): Future solution
The Lord hates sins of speech and they will be pursued to the utmost in the day of his judgment.

A[2] Problem unsolved (vv. 5–7): Unanswered prayer?
A deep sigh (verse 5a) announces that the same problem still remains: alien surroundings (verse 5b), doubt about ability to keep going (verse 6),[6] and mutual incompatibility (verse 7). So, was prayer answered after all?

See how the beginning and ending of the psalm stand in sharp contrast? In verses 1–2 the problem is, to all intents and purposes, over and done with. But no! Verses 5–7 return to the problem of verses 1–2. It has not been solved. The poor old psalmist is still as deeply in the mire as ever!

Or is he? The heart of the message of this psalm is powerful and wonderfully reassuring, a real truth for facing life. Paul wrote to the Philippians (4:6, 7) about it. The Revised Version brings out the 'in nothing . . . in everything' contrast, so here it is:

> In nothing be anxious; but in everything by prayer and supplication with thanksgiving let your requests be made known unto God. AND the peace of God, which passeth all understanding shall guard your hearts . . .

Of course, the upper case AND was my idea – to underline its importance. Paul is offering a recipe for peace; peace of heart is a by-product, a *consequence*; it arises out of prayer. When we direct our need to God ('prayer'), when we come to him in all our helplessness ('supplication'), when we take time to count our blessings with 'thanksgiving', when we simply tell him what we need ('request'), THEN we enter into a guarded and guaranteed peace. This is what Paul teaches; it is what the writer of Psalm 120 discovered. Prayer is always answered (verse 1), but, while we bide God's time (verses 5–7), the immediate consequence is that prayer, we discover, has armoured us for the daily grind.

---

### Notes

1  'World' in these verses is the Greek *kosmos*. The verb *kosmein* means 'to set in order'. The *kosmos* is this present life 'organized' to suit fallen human wisdom and values; it is 'secular society', not only finding no real place for God, but actually reckoning the very idea of God a thing of no importance or consequence (Romans 1:28). In John 17:16 Jesus says 'they (his disciples) are not of the world even as (in exactly the same way as) I am not of [the world]'. 'Of' represents the preposition *ek*, 'out of/arising from'. Like Jesus, the disciples trace their ancestry to heaven: they have been born of God (John 1:12–13).

2  The ordinary word for 'Woe (is me)' is '*oy*'. Here, for the only time in the Bible, it is developed into the longer form *oyah*.

3  NKJV 'be given . . . be done' (compare. AV, RV, NASB, ESV) interprets the verbs as 'third person singular indefinite', an idiom that invites a passive translation. The 'do . . . add' sequence uses the language of oath-taking: 'The Lord do to me, and more also' (e.g. Ruth 1:17, etc.). The NIV needlessly obscures this sequence wherever it occurs – see AV, RV, etc.

4  Why 'of the broom tree'? Commentators on the psalm suppose it to be a hard wood burning to a fierce heat. Is there evidence of this?

5  In the Bible Meshech, son of Japheth (Genesis 10:2), was known to Ezekiel as a race of inhumane businessmen (Ezekiel 27:13), warriors, uncircumcised, who caused terror to the living (32:26) and whom he

linked with Magog in the anti-God armies to be defeated at the great Day of the Lord (38:3; 39:1). Ezekiel 39:3 links them with the use of bows and arrows (compare Psalm 120:4). Kedar, second son of Ishmael (Genesis 25:13), noted for its black tents (Song of Solomon 1:5), in Isaiah (21:16,17) sharing the doom of the Gentile world – in spite of its warriors and archers (compare Psalm 120:4), but in the future rejoicing with the Gentile world over the advent of the Lord's Servant (Isaiah 42:11, compare, 42:4), and gathered into the coming glorious Zion (60:7).

6 'Too long', etc., could, with accuracy, be expressed as 'My soul has had enough of living . . . '

Psalm 121

## 4 The guarded pathway: In his world, under his shade

Psalm 121 takes up where Psalm 120 stopped. We are still in this world, but we have further discoveries to make: especially that it is *his* world. It does not belong to the worldly people, forces, pressures, threats and 'interests' that would grind us down. And also, in his world, we live under the 'shade of his hand outstretched caressingly'[1] so that we can sing with an easy mind:

> Safe in the shadow of the Lord,
> Beneath his hand and power,
> I trust in him, I trust in him,
> My fortress and my tower.[2]

### Security six times over

There is no mistaking the keynote of Psalm 121; it is sounded six times: 'he who keeps you (verse 3) . . . who keeps Israel (verse 4) . . . your keeper (verse 5) . . . will keep (verse 7) . . . will keep (verse 7) . . . will keep (verse 8).[3] That's it! That's what this psalm is all about! This is the instant answer that came to the prayer of 120:1, an answer not of extraction from life's pressures but of maintenance within them, not of the cessation of enmity as though heaven were already here and judgment already passed, but of preservation against enmity. The pilgrim path is a sheltered area, and the pilgrim a protected species.

It should go without saying, of course, that all this is a statement and a position of faith. It is like the great 'nevertheless' (NIV 'Yet') of Psalm 73:23, or the 'But even if not' of Daniel 3:18 – read them and see what I mean. We live by faith, not yet by sight (2 Corinthians 5:6–7); we are sustained by a sure and certain hope of what we do not yet have (Romans 8:24–25). We experience the slipping foot of Psalm 73:2 but we know that it is, at the same time, true that 'he will not let your foot slip' (121:3); Christian people experience all sorts of pressures, persecutions, trials, tortures and death, but it remains true, nevertheless, that 'even the very hairs of your head are all numbered' (Matthew 10:30), and 'not a hair of your head will perish' (Luke 21:18). Yes, indeed! There is a 'keeping' Lord, and we are a 'kept' people. This is our faith, the faith in which we walk our pilgrim way.

### What's your problem?

Psalm 121 opens with one question asked,[4] and another implied. The question asks 'Where does my help come from?' but this prompts another question, 'What has this got to do with lifting up our eyes to the hills?' And both questions together make us ask what it was that gave rise to this psalm before it was collected into the Songs of the Ascent.

** Was the anonymous author a resident of Jerusalem during one of the many enemy threats to the city? Imagine such a person standing on the walls, looking to the surrounding hills (Psalm 125:2), fearfully expecting at any moment to see, by day, the banners of the advancing foe, or, by night, their campfires. The eyes turned to the hills are full of dread, and the question is of the utmost urgency: Where does my help come from now?

** Or are we to think of one of the pilgrims, committed to the journey to the festival, yet knowing the dangers of travelling with a mixed and vulnerable company, passing through many a hazardous place, where hills loom and robbers lurk? What price help then? Or is the pilgrim thinking with longing of the far-off hills of Zion, and acknowledging his need for strength to reach such a distant goal? Or did the very solidity of the hills itself simply point the eye of faith beyond themselves to the greater strength of the God who is his people's Rock (Psalm 95:1 with Exodus 17:6)?

If I have not managed to spell out your favourite interpretation, forgive me, but the fact of the matter is that all such speculations represent no more than likelihood. They remain mere speculations. We do not know why the author looked to the hills or why he was prompted to ask the vital question about help. It is a situation familiar to Bible readers! We are not told all we might like to know, only what we *need* to know, and, in the present instance, the blank space is (I believe) deliberately left so that we can write in our own problems as they arise. The psalm does not offer its teaching and assurances just to a Jerusalemite of old facing whatever his problem was, or to a pilgrim of old on his particular journey. What's your problem? Look candidly at it, and then set alongside it 'the Lord, the Maker of heaven and earth (verse 2) . . . the Keeper of Israel (verse 4) . . . the Lord (who) is your shade (verse 5) . . . (able to) keep you from all harm (verse 7).' Awareness of this great sixfold keeping allows us to see our problems in their true proportions.

## The Lord the Creator (verses 1–2)

The truth about 'the Lord, the Maker of heaven and earth', as the Bible reveals him, runs far beyond merely originating everything that exists. In fact, true though that is, it is only a quarter of what the Bible teaches about God the Creator. He is, of course, the God who *began* all things (Genesis 1:1), but also he is the God who *maintains* all things in existence (e.g. Isaiah 42:5);[5] in addition he *controls* all things in their operation (e.g. Isaiah 40:26; 54:16, 17), and *directs* them to the end he has appointed (Isaiah 65:17).[6] In short, he is always in full, detailed, executive management of the world he created. He leaves nothing to chance; nothing falls outside his care and attention. Not a sparrow falls to the ground, nor is there a hair on the head of his children that he does not protect. He is God.

What a context in which to set our problems! Whatever happens happens within his world, within his purposeful working, and under his powerful rule. And this is just the starting point of what the psalm says about our security.

## The Lord the Redeemer (verses 3–4)

The psalm continues by bringing out three further aspects of our pilgrim security. First, we are guarded against the human frailty of the careless footstep (verse 3). The verb 'to give' is very versatile in Hebrew, and it often, as here, combines the two meanings of what the Lord allows and what he appoints. When it says 'he will not give your foot to slipping', it means that he will neither *intend* nor *tolerate* such a thing; it is divinely ruled out. Nothing, therefore, on the human side of pilgrimage – the exercise of walking and the hazards of picking our way along a difficult path – will be allowed to come between pilgrims and their goal. Equally, secondly, there is no lowering of the divine guard. In his care of his pilgrims the great Keeper does not 'nod off'. This is what would happen if Baal were our god (1 Kings 18:27), for it is invariably the case with any and all other gods that they are just not there when you need them! Not so the Lord. He is the ever-wakeful, watchful Guardian – guaranteed, indeed, to be so.

Thirdly, the guarantee comes in the unexpected reference to 'Israel' in verse 4. 'Israel' is the name of the Lord's firstborn son (Exodus 4:22), the son who was kept safe on the night of divine judgment (Exodus 12:12–13), when all other 'firstborn' in Egypt perished, the son whose number and needs (Exodus 12:4) were matched by the chosen lamb, and who found sheltering beneath the blood of the lamb provided full security (Exodus 12:13, 23), and found the flesh of the lamb the genuine food of pilgrims (Exodus 12:11). In effect, 'Israel' is a reminder of the Lord's work of redemption, as if to pose and answer the question: Could the Lord who redeemed his people, promising at the same time a goal to their pilgrimage in the Promised Land (Exodus 6:6–8), fail to bring them there, or forget them while they journey, or prove unfaithful to his blood-guaranteed promises?

**The Lord the Companion (verses 5–6)**

Think of well-brought-up Edwardian ladies preserving their milky complexions from the ravages of sunburn by carefully-held parasols! No good holding the parasol on your left if the sun is on the right! It has to come between the complexion and the threat. Well, then, even if this illustration fails to match the seriousness of our pilgrim situation, it perfectly pictures the grace that interposes so carefully and caringly between us and whatever threatens – whether it be the actual danger of sunstroke or the imagined danger of 'moonstroke' – for often in our poor assessment of things the imagined seems a greater threat than the actual. No matter! The Lord stands between – all round the clock, 'by day . . . by night', not holding a parasol but offering himself as our all-sufficient 'shade'.

**A comprehensive insurance policy, securely underwritten (verses 7–8)**

The divine keeping takes into account 'all harm', caters for our whole, individual, essential being,[7] covers all our activity – for all life is either going or coming, leaving home or coming home,[8] and, starting 'now', continues 'for evermore'.

The Guarantor of our comprehensive insurance cover is the God of Psalm 121, Creator, Redeemer and Companion. Have you heard of him anywhere else? Of course – the Father, the Son and the Holy Spirit! The Holy Trinity is a New Testament revelation, unrevealed before the Baptism of the Lord Jesus (Mark 1:9–11). The God revealed in the Old Testament is, however, the Holy Trinity Incognito – not, so to speak, 'just' 'God the Father', but Father, Son and Holy Spirit undeclared, unrevealed, not yet known as such. Yet so many passages allow us to see how the full New Testament revelation of the name and nature of the Godhead 'casts its shadow before it', and Psalm 121 is one of these. This is our God; this is the God of our pilgrimage. This is the God of unfailing, unending watchfulness and keeping grace, the Father, the Son and the Holy Spirit, Creator, Redeemer and Companion.

## Notes

1 From Francis Thomson, *The Hound of Heaven* (The Peter Reilly Company, 1916).

2 This beautiful hymn, by Timothy Dudley-Smith, is broadly based on Psalm 91, but could be read and pondered as an introduction to Psalm 121.

3 The NIV disturbs the keynote by offering 'watch over' in verses 3, 4, 5 and 8 and 'keep' in verse 7. Either translation is acceptable but should be maintained consistently, otherwise how can English readers arrive at a correct understanding of the topic of the psalm?

4 The AV does not treat 'from whence' as a question but as a relative clause implying that help somehow comes from the hills. This is incorrect.

5 The verbs in this verse ought to be translated in the present tense: 'creates . . . stretches . . . spreads . . . gives breath . . . ' Compare John 5:17.

6 For a fuller statement of these four aspects of the Creator's work, see Alec Motyer, *Look to the Rock* (IVP, 1996), pp. 157–161.

7 NIV 'life' is Hebrew 'soul': individual personality in its essence.

8 A lovely example of the Hebrew idiom of totality expressed by means of contrast.

Psalm 122

# 5 The pilgrim in Zion: Home at last

What a contrast! In 'the world', hostility (120:2, 6–7); in Zion, peace (122:6–8); in 'the world', alienation, unsettlement (120:5); in Zion, home, joy, delight (122:1, 9); in 'the world', isolation (120:2, 6), in Zion, fellowship (122:1, 8); on the road, dangers (121:6); in Zion, security (122:2).

**Already and not yet; yes and no**

The pilgrims have completed their journey; former woes and dreaded dangers are swallowed up in the reality of standing in the City of God (verse 2). The voice of prayer began this sequence of three psalms (120:1) and the voice of prayer concludes it (122:6). But all is transformed. The agonized prayer of the believer under pressure has become the prayer of contentment over the joys of fellowship and of the city and house of God.

Yet, though the pilgrim path has reached its destination in Zion, all is not yet as it will be some day, for Zion itself (verse 6), its security (verse 7) and its family (verse 8) are still the subjects of prayer – prayer that all that makes Zion stable may continue, and that the city itself may enjoy the peace and prosperity that keeps its fellowship rich and at ease; prayer that Yahweh's house, the central goal of pilgrimage (verse 2), may always be there to be enjoyed (verse 9).

It is in this sense that Psalm 122 is both yes and no. Our pilgrim is, like us, betwixt and between, with so much to enjoy, so much that could be threatened and lost, and so much yet to come. It is at this point that the psalm most directly addresses our situation. We too are ourselves 'aliens and strangers' (1 Peter 2:11) on earth, yet we are also already at home in Zion (Hebrews 12:22), but, equally, our enjoyment of Zion is not yet the full reality that is to come. It is at this point that the psalm speaks most directly to us. It is a truth of special importance, which needs to be explored a little further.

## Jerusalem, past, present and future

The city where the pilgrims of old arrived – Zion, Jerusalem, the City of David – lies at the beginning of one of the major 'straight lines' that run out of the Old Testament into the New, and which, like steel rods in reinforced concrete, hold the whole Bible together in its wonderful and solid unity.

### Old Jerusalem
David was the first to bring the then Jerusalem into Israelite hands and permanent occupation.[1] Did he know in advance that this was the city the Lord chose,[2] or did he realize this only afterwards? We are not told. But, looking back, we can see what an astute political masterstroke it was on David's part to unite his potentially fractious people not only around himself and his kingship, but around this new capital city, and, in time, a new residence for the Name of the Lord, a religious focal point for all the people and for every individual.[3]

When we read the books of Kings we realize to what an extent this one city dominates the narrative, and we are insensitive indeed if tears are not close at hand when we read the story of its final nincompoop king Zedekiah and of how old Jerusalem was sacked and fired by the Babylonians (2 Kings 25).

### Present Jerusalem
There is, however, another side to the story of Jerusalem. Psalm 87, for

example, foresees the day when people of all sorts will be able to claim a birthright in Zion. The psalm does not say how this will come about, except, of course, that universal rule was promised to David (Psalms 2:6–8; 89:19–27), but when we follow the straight line into the New Testament we find the answer. Paul, writing to the Galatians, made a distinction between 'the present city of Jerusalem' and 'the Jerusalem that is above', and the latter, he wrote, 'is our mother', the 'mother' of all the 'children of promise', who have been 'born by the power of the Spirit' and set free by Christ (Galatians 4:21 – 5:1). Hebrews (12:18–24) draws a contrast between the experience of darkness and fire at Sinai (Exodus 19) and the present blessedness of believers, who, it says, 'have come to Mount Zion, to the heavenly Jerusalem'. Passages that speak of our 'citizenship' belong in this context,[4] as indeed does the position of the Lord Jesus Christ as son and heir of David and himself the reigning Davidic King (Luke 1:32, 33). He reigns now; his capital city is the 'Jerusalem that is above', and the universal company of those who believe in Jesus constitutes, by birthright, its citizenry.

We need to stay with this truth a little longer. Jesus said, in a most solemn manner, that he did not come to demolish the law and the prophets but to 'fulfil' them (Matthew 5:17). 'Fulfil' is a richly flavoured idea. Think of two different sorts of plant, the annual and the perennial. An annual comes into full flower in one season, and, to put it bluntly, 'that's its lot!' Some aspects of Old Testament truth are like that. For example, in Mark 7:19 note is taken of the way Jesus brought the old food taboos to an end, declaring 'all foods clean'. They had their day, and fulfilled their purpose. They do, as a matter of fact, continue to speak to us, reminding us that, now as then,[5] our lifestyles (including our eating habits) must be a testimony to our distinctiveness as the Lord's people (Ephesians 4:1, 17; 5:1). But the specific food prohibitions as such are no longer in force.

By contrast, perennials may well flower beautifully in their first year but take a few further years to reach the maturity of beauty it is in their nature to display. Most of the Old Testament enjoys this sort of fulfilment. The sacrifices – burnt offering, peace offering and sin offering – detailed in Leviticus served their own generation but 'always had it in them' (like the bulb of a perennial) to come to a maturity of flowering in what Galatians 4:4 calls 'the time . . . fully come'. The saving work of Jesus – the cross of Calvary – is what the old sacrifices always 'had in them' and were intended to become. It is their full, and eternal, flowering. In the same way, the prophets of old, using terminology natural to them, spoke of a land yet to be possessed and a temple yet to be built,[6] but, as the New Testament teaches, the fulfilment – the full, true, and final flowering – is, in the words of Jesus, 'my kingdom . . . not of (arising out of) this world' (John 18:36), and 'the temple . . . of . . . his body' (John 2:21), now being built of 'living stones' (1 Peter 2:4, 5), as believers are gathered, worldwide, into the church (Ephesians 2:19–22). This, indeed, is also the heavenly Zion, with Jesus himself as the great 'cornerstone' on which his priestly people are being built (1 Peter 2:6–9). It is in this Zion that we, as his blood-bought people, have already arrived.

### The Jerusalem to come

Yet there is more! 'Jerusalem' is also the name of our final destiny in the New Heaven and the New Earth.[7] Indeed, in Revelation 21:9 and 10 the Bride of Christ and the city descending from heaven in all its glory are identified, a city defying all powers to describe, the eternal habitation of the Lord God and the Lamb, illuminated by their radiance, and indwelt only by those whose names are in the Lamb's Book of Life (Revelation 21:27).

## Back to the psalm

And it all started in the Jerusalem of the Old Testament. Indeed, our summary of what the whole Bible teaches about Jerusalem says nothing, in principle, that is not somehow foreshadowed in Psalm 122. The psalm makes the existing beloved city the pilgrims' goal; it dwells on the heavenly joys to be found by its members, and, by calling for prayer for this Jerusalem, it signals a future not yet realized but ardently desired. This is actually what the Psalm is 'all about'.

    $A^1$  vv. 1–2 The house and the city: Pilgrim delight
          Joy at being among those who plan pilgrimage (v. 1)
          The excitement of actually arriving (v. 2)
      B  vv. 3–5 Jerusalem's speciality: Pilgrim privileges
          Designed as a visible unity (v. 3)

The pilgrim target of Yahweh's tribes (v. 4a)
Joined in obedience ('statute'), for worship ('praise')
(v. 4b)
Under the rule and protection of the house of David
(v. 5)
A² vv. 6–9 The city and the house: Pilgrim prayer
Topics for prayer (vv. 6–7)
Peace and prosperity for city and people (v. 6)
Peace and prosperity within a strong city (v. 7)
Grounds for prayer (vv. 8–9)
Delight in family fellowship (v. 8)
Delight in Yahweh's house (v. 9)

## Our interim Jerusalem

How easily, then, we can identify with this psalm. In the dim, distant
past, we used to sing a hymn with the chorus lines:

> We're marching to Zion, beautiful, beautiful Zion!
> We're marching upwards to Zion, the beautiful City of God![8]

Antiquated? Certainly . . . True? Oh yes! That is our goal, and the more
we set our minds on it, the more enthusiastically we will march on; the
more we long for it, the more zealously we will live as if already there
(which, in the truest sense, we are);[9] the more we dwell on its glories
and on the beauty of its King, the more our hearts will be set on holiness; the more we bring the coming New Heaven and Earth and the
ascended Christ into our thinking the more we will live as New Earth
people in this old world. People around us may talk about being so
heavenly minded that we are no earthly use. Bible in hand, we turn
their mockery on its head, for it is only those who have pilgrimage
in their hearts who know how to live this earthly life (Psalm 84:5–6); the
goal of the Jerusalem to come, the New Heaven and the New Earth,
the City of the Lord God and of the Lamb, casts its radiance before it
for those who live in its light; the values of the city that is yet to be arm
us for living in the city that is now.

Or, to put it another way, our pilgrim *goal* is also our daily *task*. We are on our way to Zion, but we have already come to Zion – and, importantly, to its present location in the local church to which we belong.

When we see even the slightest sliver of a crescent moon, we don't say, 'Oh look, there's part of the moon'; we say, 'Oh, look, there's the moon.' In exactly the same way, our aim should be that whoever looks at even the tiniest, most insignificant, struggling church should be not only able but compelled to say, 'Oh look, there's the New Jerusalem.'

** *Where problems are solved.* This is the point at which our thoughts on Psalm 122 began (page 38 above), but it deserves to be recalled. In 'the world' there is adversity (120:1), enmity (120:2), verbal sniping (120:3), deep unsettlement (120:5), antagonism to the ways of peace (120:6, 7). In the church there is delighted fellowship, family feeling (122:1, 8), a sense of security (122:2), delight in peace and in speaking peace (122:6, 8). The church is a place where the problems of the world are solved – and this is not just an essential of our testimony to the watching world, it is for our own enjoyment and healing. It is, of course, what the world needs to see – for why should anyone want to join a church not worth joining, a company beset by the very problems a person wants to be rid of? But, at the deepest level, it is what believers themselves need: a secure, restful, curative fellowship, a 'time out' from the world, not, negatively, an escapist withdrawal, but, positively, a 'recharging of batteries'.

** *Where love and peace predominate and preoccupy.* The fellowship, mutuality and family-oneness of the Lord's people run like a plaited cord through Psalm 122. In verse 1 the frequent translation 'when they said to me' (NKJV, NASB, ESV, etc.) is unsupported by Hebrew usage.[10] The psalmist is not rejoicing over an occasion but over people: 'I rejoiced over those who were saying to me, "To Yahweh's house we will go".' Well, just imagine it: the psalmist is in the situation described in Psalm 120, feeling down, friendless, isolated and alienated, longing for peace, facing animosity, and along come a group with plans laid to go on pilgrimage to Zion! Not only that, but also, on arriving in Jerusalem, the very design of the city speaks of unity (verse 3). They look around them and see 'the tribes of the Lord', the Lord's very own people (verse 4),[11] together in obedience and worship (verse 4b), owning the same king (verse 5), loving the same city (verse 6), and belonging to each other as 'brothers and friends' (verse 8). Their unity is not something they hope to attain. It is the given reality of the city of which they are citizens, and of the family in which they are sons and daughters.

\*\* *A church united round God's word* (verse 4b), *God's name* (verse 4b) *and God's house* (verse 9). In verse 4b 'statute' is, literally, 'testimony'. Israel is the people marked out by revelation, by possessing the word of a God who has borne 'testimony', revealing himself and his requirements. They know his 'Name' – the revealed 'shorthand' that comprises all that he has made known about himself. When they made pilgrimage they did so in obedience to his word; and when they worshipped they gave first place (not to their needs, or their likes and dislikes but) to the revealed nature of their God.[12] Furthermore, what makes Jerusalem the pilgrims' goal is 'the house of the Lord our God' (verse 9), the place where he has graciously come to live among his people, and where the sacrifices he has commanded make it possible for them to 'draw near' to him. These are the three central realities of true worship: the word of God, his revealed character, and the atoning blood.

\*\* *A reigning King and a praying people* (verses 5, 6–9). The Davidic king was the lynchpin of the whole arrangement. It was he who provided and guaranteed the stability of the kingdom and the continuation of city and house as the goal for pilgrims. In the old city, how important it was, then, to acknowledge the presence and ruling rights of the king (verse 5), and to pray for his continued prospering and strength (verses 6–7). Without the king within and the walls around, there would be nothing to come to, no buildings displaying cohesion, no safe place of fellowship. So they encouraged each other to pray for these things – a reigning king upholding what is right, a prosperous community protected by strong walls.[13] In other words, nothing much changes: the church should still be known and developed as a place of prayer – that Christ may reign, that peace and prosperity may prevail, that the church continue in strength – prayers prompted by concern for the well-being of the family of God (verse 8) and for the maintenance of the good news of the atonement (verse 9).

\*\* *The individual and the cause of peace.* At the start of the psalm, we meet an individual rejoicing in fellowship (verse 1, see above), and the psalm ends with that same individual calling for prayer (verse 6), and stating first to pray for peace. If our churches fall short of the ideal the psalm sketches, is it because we each, as individuals, have fallen short in our personal devotion to peace and prayer?

## Notes

1  The incoming tribe of Judah 'took' Jerusalem but did not seek to hold it (Judges 1:8–9). David – contrary to what anyone thought possible – captured and occupied the city (2 Samuel 5:6–9; 1 Chronicles 11:4–8).

2  Deuteronomy 12:5, 11; 1 Kings 8:44.

3  Note the anxieties of Jeroboam, the rebel king who founded the northern state of Israel and divided David's kingdom, about what would result if the people continued to make pilgrimage to Jerusalem (1 Kings 12:26–27).

4  E.g. Ephesians 2:11–13; Philippians 1:27 (literally, 'live as citizens'); 3:20.

5  Deuteronomy 14: the chapter begins by announcing its theme (verses 1–2), the distinctiveness of the children of the Lord.

6  E.g. Ezekiel 36:24–30; Amos 9:11–15; Ezekiel 40 – 48.

7  Compare Isaiah 65:17–25; Revelation 21 – 22.

8  By Isaac Watts, 'Come, ye that love the Lord', *Golden Bells*, 31.

9  Ephesians 4:2–6; Hebrews 12:22.

10  There is no question about this. When an occasion is in mind, the verb ($\sqrt{samach}$) requires the preposition *b* with an infinitive verb (e.g. Psalm 105:38; Proverbs 24:17), but *b* with a noun or pronoun – or, as here, a participle – specifies that which causes the joy.

11  The addition 'the tribes of the Lord' is no mere poetic flourish. It is making a point. The people crowding into Jerusalem ('the tribes go up') are not a chance aggregation; they are 'Yahweh's tribes', his very own people congregating to worship.

12  The NIV reverses the order of lines in verse 4b. 'According to statute' should come first, followed (more properly) by 'to give thanks to the name'. The word of God must always be the primary reality, even in the place of worship. Worship concentrates on what the Lord has done, prompting thanksgiving, and keeps his name, the truth he has revealed about himself, right in the foreground.

13  We need to remember that 'judgment' is one of the words the Old Testament uses for God's revealed truth (often translated 'laws' in the

NIV, e.g. Deuteronomy 5:1). Moses appointed 'judges' (Deuteronomy
1:15, 16) so that the people could be governed by the Lord's revealed
truth, right down to the ordinary household ('tens'). The task of
'judging' is of setting everything to rights in the light of God's word.
'Peace' is 'well-being' in all the areas and aspects of life – peace with
God, in society and in the heart.

Psalm 123

## 6 At the end of our tether: The Lord above

The central thought of Psalm 123 is so beautifully simple to state: at the end of our tether there's a place called Prayer.

### Small room, quiet voice

It's a place easy to overlook, dreadfully easy to avoid, all too easy to scorn, a place of quietness and restful reassurance, but also a place calling for patient durability, one of the little places of earth, a secret cherished between the soul and the Lord. It is infinitely easier to moan about our lot, and to commiserate with ourselves – to turn yet again to solutions that the past has proved ineffective. But the little place, the easily unnoticed and avoided place remains; its door is open; and from inside a most loving voice invites, saying, 'Come to me and rest.'

That voice will most certainly address us again when we come to Psalm 131, though actually it is the pervasive 'incidental music' to the whole book of 'pilgrim praise', but, specially, when we read Psalm 123, our thoughts go back to Psalm 120 where we started. Have we not moved forward at all? Is our pilgrim path stuck in a sort of rut of discomfort and opposition? Well, yes! Our march to Zion is always, as

Bunyan wrote, 'through the wilderness of this world'.[1] We need to beware of ever thinking otherwise. It is always 'through the night of doubt and sorrow' that 'onward goes the pilgrim band',[2] and any voice that says otherwise is a siren voice! But equally always the small open door accompanies us, with its invitation to meet our hazards in faith and prayer.

Is Psalm 123 any different, then, from Psalm 120? The situation is, in principle, much the same (120:6; 123:3, 4),[3] and in each case is met by prayer. The emphasis, however, in 120 is that prayer brings immediate consolation and fortitude. In other words, Psalm 120 underlines the prompt fortification of spirit that prayer brings. By contrast, in 123 we see that prayer takes it for granted that the answer to the outward problem is sure to come, and settles down to wait for it. Matching these different nuances, Psalm 120 centres on the awesome power of the Lord dealing in judgment with his and our foes (verses 3–4); Psalm 123 centres on the Lord's threefold 'mercy . . . mercy . . . mercy', overshadowing us in our time of trial and of waiting.

### (1) The place called 'Prayer' (verse 1)

The psalmist has reached saturation point in his sensitivity to the contemptuous and mocking behaviour of those around him (verses 3–4) but he wants us to know that in a trice this can be exchanged for a one-to-one, even in its way a face-to-face or eye-to-eye, relationship with the enthroned God (verse 1). All we have to do is look up!

Prayer, says the hymn, is 'the upward glancing of an eye, when none but God is near'.[4]

The Lord Jesus Christ knew how to slip into this quiet room with his Father. In John 13 – 16 he had been speaking about the his own 'going away', i.e. to the cross (John 13:33), knowing in detail, as he did, everything that it entailed (John 18:4); he had spoken about the arrival of Satan in all his power (14:30), about the world's hatred of him (15:18), about how he would be deserted and left by himself (16:32), and of much else that puts him well in the context of Psalm 123. We read (John 17:1, literally) that: 'Jesus said these things, and, lifting up his eyes to heaven, he said, "Father, . . . " ' What a perfect illustration of Psalm 123:1.

But how can the mere uplifting of the eye be sufficient? It is so unobtrusive, so easily unnoticed. It is not like waving a hand or a banner, or like shouting out loud. No, the uplifted eye is effective only if it connects with another eye already looking down. This is the picture the psalm paints for us. In the misery of his situation the psalmist looks up. Just then, at the end of his tether, that's all he seems able to manage. But, wonder of wonders, he looks up to discover that the Lord has never stopped looking down, and is there, waiting for their eyes to meet. He is rightly called 'You who hear prayer' (Psalm 65:2); it is his nature to be alert for prayer, to maintain an unflinching gaze in readiness for the uplifted eye of his needy ones.

## The God of Heaven

Michael Wilcock notices how applicable this psalm is to the situation of Nehemiah in Jerusalem, facing, as he did, the strongest opposition of local magnates.[5] This may very well be the point at which the psalm originated, before its incorporation in 'Pilgrim Praise'. It is a special link that Nehemiah makes his recurrent appeal to 'the God of heaven'. He is the God to whom to bring the most impossible tasks and the deepest sorrows (Nehemiah 1:2–5), to whom we may appeal when even the supreme powers on earth have to be turned this way or that (Nehemiah 2:2–4), and who may be relied on to see us through when we face triumphalist mockery (Nehemiah 2:19–20).

And all that is needed is the 'upward glancing of an eye', for our upward look meets the downward gaze of the One 'whose throne is in heaven'. This translation spotlights one of three possible meanings: the Lord 'sits' in heaven (RV), his 'home' is in heaven (JerB), and he is 'enthroned' in heaven (NIV, NASB). Each meaning adds its own 'dimension' to the place called 'Prayer'. Coming there, we set aside the troubles and toils of the world and enter a place of rest, where he 'sits'; we turn from our poverty and want into his 'home', where there is everything in abundance, his 'riches in glory' (Philippians 4:19, NKJV); and we bring our powerlessness in the face of stronger forces and overwhelming odds into the place of power where he is king. The storms of earth are not storms in heaven, where all is at rest; the wants of earth are swamped by the ocean flood of heaven's resources; and the forces and oppositions of earth do not count in heaven, where real sovereignty is enthroned.

## (2) Laying burdens down (verse 2a)

In the symbolism of the Old Testament the eye is the organ of desire, and the hand is the organ of 'intervention' and personal action. This is the next 'prayer picture' of Psalm 123. We come submitting our needs (eyes) to his decisions (hand). It is our job to wait, his to act. The place of prayer is the place of submission, because that is our status. We are the servants, he the master; we the maidservants, he the mistress. The contrasts of masculine and feminine and of plural with singular are Hebrew idioms of totality. In other words, there is no exception to this 'rule' in the place of prayer. It is so always and for everyone: 'May your will be done' (Matthew 26:42). Our status as servants demands it, and so does our condition as those who, without merit or deserving, are crying out for mercy. The word (*chanan*) is the Old Testament equivalent to the New Testament grace, and has exactly the same meaning. We come as those without merit: there is nothing about us to attract the favours we seek; we come without deserving: we have done and can do nothing to earn what we need. It is all about mercy, all about grace.

## (3) Waiting with patience; waiting with confidence (verse 2b)

Small words must not be overlooked! The simplicity of the upward gaze (verse 1) must be matched by its patient, servant-like[6] continuance 'till' mercy arrives, for even the most urgent prayer must learn to submit itself to the Lord's timetable.[7] Psalm 120:1 rejoiced in an answer coming immediately; the parallel in 123:2 is a call for persistence. The simplicity of asking runs on a parallel line with the discipline of seeking and the patience of knocking (Luke 11:9–10).

Look at Genesis 16 and learn the mischief that arises out of impatience when Abram and Sarai could not submit to the Lord's timetable! Look at Exodus 32. When we grow impatient we are prone to make golden calves, and debase the coinage of the Lord's unique glory!

Verse 2, however, helps us to exercise the necessary patience (Hebrews 6:12). The formal title, 'you whose throne is in heaven' of verse 1, becomes 'Yahweh our God', the LORD,[8] known by name and personally claimed. This is deeply significant. The Lord first revealed the meaning of his personal name, Yahweh, through Moses to Israel at a time when their subordinate status in Egypt had actually become slavery. It was this people he chose and delivered and brought to himself. It was by this Exodus action, says David (2 Samuel 7:23), that the Lord 'made a name for himself'. With what supreme confidence, then, can his current helpless ones, likewise at the end of their tether, make their appeal for mercy! He desires to be known for ever (Exodus 3:15) by the name that proclaims that he loved his slaves and loves them still. If he seems to delay the answer to our urgency, he is under no obligation to 'explain himself' to us. Maybe he expects us to remember what he said to Peter: 'You do not realize now what I am doing, but later you will understand' (John 13:7). More likely he will put John 11:5–6 into our minds: 'Jesus loved Martha and her sister and Lazarus. Yet (literally, 'Therefore') when he heard that Lazarus was sick, he stayed where he was two more days.' Why? Not, certainly, through any lack of love! 'Yahweh' is the God who 'loves us because he loves us' (Deuteronomy 7:7–8).

### (4) Prayer, the place where we matter (verse 3)

So far, Psalm 123 has based its praying on *what* God is and *who* God is: he is the One enthroned in heaven (verse 1), and he is Yahweh, the lover of his downtrodden people (verse 2). It now offers a third, and most significant, ground on which we can lift our prayerful eyes to the throne: 'for we . . .' (verse 3). We rest on his power and resources as the enthroned God; we pray confidently for mercy because of his love for us (Ephesians 2:4); but we may also come before him simply to plead our personal need.

O Saviour, I have nought to plead,
In earth around or heaven above,
But just my own exceeding need
And thy exceeding love.[9]

The Lord our God does not change. Why did he, long ago, bother about his people in Egypt? 'I have seen the misery of my people . . . I have heard them crying out . . . I am concerned about their suffering . . . I have come down to rescue them' (Exodus 3:7, 8). In prayer we cannot tell him anything he does not know already: before we cry out he has seen our misery; he actually feels our pain – literally, 'I know their sorrows'; and he comes to us himself, willing and able to deliver.

## (5) At the end of out tether, there's a place called 'Prayer' (verses 3–4): Prayer as counter-attack

Prayer as such is a very simple thing, as simple as looking up. Also, the place of prayer is always accessible. It doesn't require a journey, or even a bodily movement, just a redirection of mind and of the inward voice. As well as all this, we know that the place of prayer is a benediction, once we get there. So why is it that so often our own reluctance is so powerful? Now there's a mystery! The need is great, the solution is simple, the hesitation is obstinate. So often it is just so, and for so many of us.

The psalm says nothing about this. It shows us the effective reality of the uplifted eye, and offers us the example of intercession in its simple essentials. It is we who have to recognize that – alas, so very often – the remedy is there but the spoonful of remedial medicine hovers between bottle and mouth. We find it easier to talk to ourselves about our miseries than to look up with the reliant, persistent, patient gaze of servant and maid. We would do more than well, then, to listen to this lovely psalm. It is not a stick but a carrot, fresh and succulent, tempting us into the place where the burden that has almost exhausted our strength can be laid down.

### The exhaustion factors

The NIV translation 'much . . . much . . . ' is accurate but possibly not forceful enough. The construction can carry the 'implication of excess',[10] and that is more suitable here: 'We are more than sated / We have had more than our fill' (verse 3), and verse 4 could be rendered, 'Our soul has had more than its fill . . . ' The reference to 'soul' indicates that the problem has penetrated into the very heart of the person. Four aspects are mentioned:

** 'Contempt', 'to treat as of no consequence' (as 'despises', 2 Kings 19:21); As when people say things like, 'What you hold dear, no thoughtful person could possibly believe.'
** 'Ridicule': 'mockery' and 'derision' put into words, made a laughing matter; 'You don't really believe that, do you? What a joke!'
** 'The proud', better 'the complacent', those who are 'at ease with themselves', in the bad sense of being devoid of moral seriousness, dismissive of standards, or of any thought of the supernatural or of divine judgment to come; 'What's all this talk about sin and judgment? I don't hurt anyone; "Why bother?" I say. I'm certainly as good as anyone else and better than most!'
** 'The arrogant', literally 'high, lofty', those who look down on others as from a great height, the 'superior'; they know better, have greater insight, can put everyone else right. '*You* can't face life without praying about it. *Me*? I can handle it!'

How Egyptian contemporaries would have mocked the thought that the blood of a lamb could effect salvation! When a people is under threat of genocide, isn't 'take a lamb' (Exodus 12:3) just pathetic? And today Bible-believing Christians hold the blood of Jesus precious, accept his miracles, believe him to be both God and Man, one Person, proclaim that his death is 'one sacrifice for sins for ever' (Hebrews 10:12, NKJV), rejoice in an empty tomb and a bodily resurrection, affirm that he ascended visibly into heaven, that he sits enthroned above all, that he will return visibly as he went (Acts 1:11), that we shall be caught up to meet him in the air (1 Thessalonians 4:17), to stand before the judgment seat of Christ (2 Corinthians 5:10), and to enjoy for ever the New Heaven and the New Earth (Revelation 21 – 22). The scornful will still scorn, the mockers mock, the intellectual snobs dismiss, and the self-confident go their self-satisfied way. Consequently we must let Psalm 123 speak to us. We will not be left unmolested, nor escape unscathed. For us too the only resource is the uplifted eye, for our God still reigns.

## Notes

1 *Pilgrim's Progress*, Everyman Edition (Dent, 1937), p. 6.
2 'Through the night of doubt and sorrow', B. S. Ingemann, *Hymns of Faith*, 519.
3 The Hebrew construction in these verses has greater similarity than the English allows. Maybe just to make 123:3, 4 read 'too much . . . too much' would help.
4 'Prayer is the soul's sincere desire', James Montgomery, *Hymns of Faith*, 455.
5 M. Wilcock, *The Message of Psalms*, Two Vols, The Bible Speaks Today (IVP, 2001), Vol. 2, pp. 227, 228. Note, for example, the same vocabulary of mockery and scorn: Nehemiah 2:19; 4:4 <3:26>.
6 The NIV, verse 2, offers 'slaves', but there is no Hebrew word for 'slave/slavery', only the words for 'servant/servanthood'. Servanthood can so easily degenerate into slavery, of course, but the Old Testament was careful to set up safeguards, notably the requirement that every male in a household must be circumcised (e.g. Genesis 17:13, i.e. brought into the covenant family and given the privileges and protections of the covenant. It is noteworthy that the first situation requiring case law was when a servant had no desire, after the period of his servanthood, to leave his master (Exodus 21:2–6). Female servants, lacking the safeguard of circumcision, were the subject of special protective laws (e.g. Exodus 21:7–11). In the present verse, the parallelism with 'maid (-servant, *shiphchah*) should have been sufficient to rule out the 'translation' 'slaves'.
7 In verse 1 'I lift' is actually a Hebrew 'perfect' tense. It represents here a fixed attitude, deliberately adopted. 'I set myself to lift'; 'I stand with eyes lifted'.
8 It is always important, not least in Psalms, to remember that when the English versions use four upper-case letters, LORD, this stands for the divine Name, Yahweh.
9 J. Crewdson, Chorus 505, *CSSM Choruses No. 2*, Children's Special Service Mission, 1935.
10 BDB, p. 913a, e.g. Genesis 45:28, 'That's enough!' (NIV 'I'm convinced'); Better Deuteronomy 3:26; see also Psalm 120:6, NIV 'Too long'.

Psalm 124

## 7 Against overwhelming odds: The Lord alongside

Do you know the word 'to extrapolate', all eleven letters of it? It means to take conclusions reached in one situation and apply them to another, maybe as an experiment, to see if they work, or – in the case of this psalm – to transplant truths learned in one set of circumstances into a different (and, here, larger) setting.

It's not as complicated as it sounds! At its heart Psalm 124 refers poetically to four potentially life-threatening dangers. In verse 3 the most direct reference is to an earthquake, such as actually happened in Numbers 16:31–33, but in personal or national life a similar danger, threatening total extinction, can come through human hostility or circumstantial threat – like the ground opening up to swallow us. A second danger within the physical realm is depicted in verse 4. Palestine abounded in what are properly called 'winterbournes', riverbeds full of water in the rainy seasons, but dry at other times. An unexpected heavy rainfall in the hills would send flash floods rushing down, and the dry channel would suddenly become a raging torrent, and woe betide anything or anybody caught in its path. The psalm speaks of 'raging waters', using the verb 'to boil', referring not to heat but to swirling, destructive turbulence.

David now turns to two examples of danger drawn from the animal kingdom. First (verse 6), there is the savage beast, with teeth to tear flesh and shatter bone, and, finally (verse 7), there is the hidden menace of the cunningly placed trap, well baited to lure the unwary bird.

In these ways the world around us is full of menace. In the Old Testament, to double a thing expresses certainty or fixity (cf. Genesis 41:32), and here we have two illustrations from the physical environment (earthquake and flood), and two from the animal environment (the prowling beast and the ensnared bird); and, as we have seen before, contrast is a Hebrew way of expressing totality. Whether we think in terms of physical geography or of the animal creation, there is no place we are free of threat, no place where we are free to relax our guard.

## David's outlaw days

David must have felt the ground opening up under his feet (verse 3) many a time during the days when he went in fear for his life because of Saul. When, for example, he entered Keilah to rescue people he supposed to be friendly from a Philistine attack, he suddenly realized that the very walls and gates that kept the Philistines out locked him in (1 Samuel 23:7)! Oh, yes, he could send the Philistines packing, but he had 'painted himself into a corner'! Saul was on his triumphant way, thinking that David was, at last, easy prey! Or, again, did David not face an all-engulfing threat (verses 4–5) when nothing but a ridge of hill separated him from Saul's encircling troops (1 Samuel 23:25, 26)? The enemy forces would be over the skyline at any moment, roaring down on him! In the same way, the paranoiac hatred of the king could well have seemed to David's poetic imagination like the snarling of a savage beast (verse 6) as he recalled Saul reaching for his spear (1 Samuel 19:9, 10) – maybe even also actual prowling of lions around his lonely cave (Psalm 57: 4). Then again, there was a hidden snare (verse 7) by the name of Doeg the Edomite with his opportunist ear cocked to overhear David being creative with the truth (1 Samuel 21:7; 22:22) – and how many other traps well baited, who can tell, during those desperate days of self-imposed outlawry (Psalm 142:3)?

## Extrapolation

Yes, there's that word again! David looked back, and, poetically speaking, saw how he had been threatened by the earthquake experience of ground opening up and swallowing him, by flash floods, by wild beasts on the prowl, and by cunningly-baited traps well concealed (compare 1 Samuel 18:21, 25). They were all there in his fugitive days, but now, as king, he turns them into a lesson for his people, for those same dangers are part and parcel of life in this dangerous world in which the Lord's people are set. For them too the very next step might seem to take them into the yawning pit; they too will struggle to keep their heads above the raging waters, to escape the teeth of savage foes, and to extricate their feet from mantraps. They need to be alert to the realities of the world around, and to know the solution he found, the security he proved to be sufficient.

## David's teaching

The establishment of David's infant kingdom did not pass unnoticed by its neighbours. Saul was far from being an inconsiderable ruler, but by the time he himself came to the throne David had already proved his abilities as soldier and statesman, and, for example, both the Philistines and the Edomites were on the alert for an opportunity to nip the blossoming kingdom in the bud. The Philistine Wars are recorded in 2 Samuel 5:17–25. We need to remember that the Bible does not tell us all we might like to know, or all there was to know, only what we need to know. We might, therefore, form the mistaken impression that this fight with the Philistines was no more than a border skirmish, of no great significance. But look at verses 17, 18 and 25. It was the news that David had become king that roused the Philistines to battle, and their aim was 'to search' for David, putting an end to his kingship before it had properly started. Their armies penetrated as far as Rephaim, near Jerusalem[1] itself.

The Edomite Wars are alluded to in 2 Samuel 8:14 but the seriousness of the situation can be inferred from Psalm 60.[2] David, behaving like a stereotypical king ('Have army, will make war'), invaded the northern kingdom of Hadadezer (2 Samuel 8:4) while the latter was away fighting on his own northern borders. Meanwhile, catching David with his back turned, Edom invaded Judah from the south. It actually served David right for gratuitously going to war in the interests of making a territorial acquisition, but, nonetheless, a successful Edomite invasion would have obliterated the little more than embryo kingdom.

Was David ever out of 'hot water'? Yet it was in 'hot water', whether in his fugitive days or his kingly days, that he harvested some of his most precious lessons, which, by way of 'extrapolation', he applied poetically in Psalm 124 to national emergencies – and which we in turn can 'extrapolate' in order to arm ourselves for the knocks and shocks of life. There is still the day when the ground seems to open under our feet, or yawn like a great pit in front of us; trouble still rushes suddenly up on us, threatening to engulf us; people are no 'nicer' now than then, and there are still enemies like marauding predators; and, as if these were not enough, traps and snares await the unwary foot. If you are not somewhere in this catalogue today, possibly you were yesterday, and more than likely you will be tomorrow! Since we can, in this way, reckon David's *troubles* are ours, can we extrapolate his *remedies* too?

## The 'clothes line' of Psalm 124

How often it is the case that, if we puzzle out the structure or 'shape' of a psalm, its message immediately stares us in the face! Look at Psalm 124:

$A^1$  vv. 1–2 The Lord alongside
  $B^1$  vv. 3–5 Deliverance against all odds
            Two examples of circumstantial dangers

$A^2$  v. 6a The Lord in sovereign control
  $B^2$  vv. 6b–7 Total deliverance
      vv. 6b–7a Two examples of 'animal' dangers
      v. 7b The danger itself ended: the snare broken
$A^3$  v. 8 The Lord of All

Most of the psalm is occupied with the dangers on the pilgrim way – as befits its place as the second psalm in its group of three, matching

Psalm 121. But, as clothes on a line are held in place by clothes pegs, three strong pegs are the real message of the psalm. It is not only a psalm of our problems (B$^{1,2}$) – though they are clearly acknowledged and firmly faced; it is a psalm of solutions (A$^{1,2,3}$), a recipe for daily living in the face of problems.

### (1) The constancy of the Lord in the realm of grace (verse 1)

Verses 1 and 2 are 'parallel', a literary form familiar in the Psalms. They both declare that the Lord is 'on our side', but to be parallel is not to be identical. The first verse states the truth in its simplicity; the second, as we shall see, has something to add.

As we go on our pilgrimage, then, the fact is that we never walk alone; we are always accompanied. The Lord who is with us is also 'for us', not only 'at our side' but '*on* our side' (compare 121:5). Think of Luke 24:15, 'Jesus himself came up and walked along with them'.[3] They did not recognize their Companion, and it is often like this: our feeling is that we are alone; we have prayed, but see no answer; we long for the comfort of the Lord's presence, but seem condemned to walk alone. Not so! Never so! 'The Lord is on our side.' Time will prove what feelings have doubted; hindsight will correct blindness. He never leaves or forsakes (Hebrews 13:5) those who are his chosen children – his 'Israel'.

This is the point of David's cry 'Oh let Israel say!'[4] They are 'Israel', those whom the Lord adopted as his firstborn son (Exodus 4:22), the people of the blood of the lamb (Exodus 12:12, 13), the Lord's pilgrims (Exodus 12:11). They are our forebears in grace, and we who are 'Israel' in Christ (Galatians 3:29; 6:16) inherit and rest on the Israel promises of God. Those who are saved by grace (Ephesians 2:4–8) are given the guarantee of being eternally safeguarded. It was for us he gave his only Son, and with him he freely gives all things (Romans 8:32), including the unfailing presence of the unchanging Jesus (Hebrews 13:5–6, 8).

### (2) The superiority of the Lord in the realm of power (verse 2)

We now come to the parallel verse 2. Verse 1 starts with 'the LORD' and ends (the last word in the Hebrew) with 'Israel'. Thus the balance of the sentence holds together the Lord and the people saved by grace, preparing the ground for the guarantee of constant favour whereby the Lord is always on the side of his chosen ones. Verse 2 starts with 'the LORD' and ends (the last word in the Hebrew) with 'men', more particularly, *'adam,* 'humankind' in its creatureliness. To amplify this thought we can either look forward to Hebrews 13:6 or back to the source of the Hebrews quotation in Psalm 118:6. The Creator has all power over the creature; the creature has no power against the Creator. It is in this way that, while verse 1 focuses on grace, its parallel, verse 2, moves the focus to power. The proper development of this thought must await our consideration of verse 8, and is best left for the moment, but the central emphasis of verse 2 – and the comfort and confidence it brings to the Lord's pilgrims – must not be deferred. Our pilgrim path always lies in the arena of his power; the power on our side is superior to all the power of the enemy (Luke 10:19); 'the one who is in you is greater than the one who is in the world' and 'this is the victory that has overcome the world, even our faith' (1 John 4:4; 5:4).

### (3) *The authority of the Lord in the realm of decision (verse 6)*
Two issues of translation arise in verse 6, and a comparison of the NIV with the NKJV shows what they are. Where the NIV offers 'praise be', the NKJV has 'blessed be'; and where the NIV translates 'who has not let', the NKJV puts 'who has not given'. Each of the four is allowable, but important nuances emerge as we try to get nearer to what David is saying.

Basically, there is no doubt that 'blessed be' is more accurate than 'praise be'. A distinct word within the vocabulary of worship is involved, and it is the same word we use in order to seek God's 'blessing' for ourselves or our friends.[5] 'To 'bless' God has, therefore, its own subtle shade of meaning. When we ask God to bless a friend, we are unconsciously using shorthand. If we spelled out our prayer, it would be something like this: 'Lord, please review their needs and meet them.' When we 'bless' God, we are again using a shorthand. He has no needs but he has revealed his nature, his character and his glory. To bless God is to review what he is, to bring his glories to mind, and to respond in wonder, worship and adoration. To 'praise' God calls to mind what he has done; to bless him calls to mind what he is.

And what, in particular, calls forth 'blessing' in verse 6? The verb 'to give' ($\sqrt{natan}$) is extremely versatile in Hebrew use: to put, place, appoint, grant, allow – all these are well exemplified. The NIV 'let' is, therefore, fully permissible. Nevertheless, the basic meaning of the verb is to give, speaking not simply of divine permission but much more of divine decision or direction. In any and every situation, not least – maybe even especially – when danger threatens, the decision on how we shall fare rests not with our adversaries (however sharp their teeth) but with our God. We look up to him as the Bible reveals him and we worship before a God who is really and truly God. To him belong the throne and the right to rule, and it is he who settles the issue, directs the experience, and decides the outcome. To have faced and come out unscathed from some potentially life-threatening situation (as in verse 6) is not down to our cleverness, or even our worthiness, but to his directive will.

### (4) The sovereignty of the Lord in the realm of creation (verse 8)[6]

We come now to the climax of the revelation of the Lord on which this psalm hangs. He is on our side in grace (verse 1), and in superior power (verse 2); his is that authoritative, decision-making power that appoints our experiences (verse 6). Finally, his power extends in sovereign executive control over all things in heaven and earth (verse 8), for he is God the Creator.

### The fourfold power of the Creator

When we speak of God as Creator, usually our attention is preoccupied with Genesis 1 and the fact that he is the originator and beginning of everything, the One who in majesty speaks and it is done, commands and they are created (Psalm 33:6–9). But there is much, much more. In Genesis 2:4 onwards, the Lord God demonstrates that he is sovereign over the humans he created: he did not ask Adam if he wanted to be a gardener; he made the garden and put the man there – just like that! He did not consult Adam on whether he wished to marry or remain single; he immobilized him in sleep and Adam awoke a married man. We move on to Genesis 3 where Eve and Adam succumb to the alluring tempter, but when the Lord God enters the garden it is with unimpaired sovereignty. Even the great rebellion itself leaves God still on the throne! It is he who declares to Adam and Eve what their new, deteriorated condition means (3:16–19); it is he who banishes them from the garden and makes it impossible for them, of themselves, to return (3:22–24); it is he who pledges the coming blessedness of deliverance from the serpent's usurpation (3:15); and, maybe most remarkable of all, the hitherto voluble serpent is totally silent before God.

In this simple way the Genesis narrative teaches a great truth: the Creator is sovereign Lord of his creation. He initiates all things (Genesis 1:1), maintains them in existence (Isaiah 42:5),[7] controls them in operation (e.g. Isaiah 40:26; 54:16, 17), and directs them to their appointed end (e.g. Isaiah 65:17, 18).

How great he is, then, and how great his power! It is this God who is on our side, and it is in his world that we live, walk our pilgrim way, and meet the experiences of life. Yet our relationship goes beyond that of creature to Creator. 'Our help,' says David, 'is in the name of the LORD' (verse 8a). Wherever we read of his 'name' our minds should at once fly back to Exodus 3:15. His 'name' declares who and what he is: he is the Lord who came to Egypt to save us when we were helpless and hopeless, and who, in doing so, revealed himself to us, his chosen children (Exodus 4:22) and his redeemed (Exodus 6:6). He is our God for ever and ever, our Guide even to death (Psalm 48:14).[8]

---

## Notes

1 J. Baldwin, *1, 2 Samuel*, TOTC (IVP, 1988), p. 203, 'The Valley of Rephaim is within sight of Jerusalem . . . to the south-west'.

2 See Alec Motyer, *Treasures of the King* (IVP, 2007), pp. 106–108.

3 AV, RV, NKJV strike a movingly emotive chord: 'Jesus himself drew near and went with them.'

4 'Now' (AV, NKJV, RV, ESV) must be judged a mistranslation. The particle *na'* does not express 'time when' but is used to strengthen an appeal, to express the idea 'please', etc. Hence 'Oh, please, may Israel say', i.e. may they ever react, whenever the time demands, in the light of the Lord's unfailing identification with them.

5 √*barak*, noun b'*rakah*. In Genesis 1:28, God 'blessed them'; in 24:31 Laban calls Jacob 'blessed of the Lord'.

6 See A Motyer, *Look to the Rock* (IVP, 1996).

7 The verbs in this verse are participles, expressing what is going on all the time. On the fourfold understanding of God the Creator, again see A. Motyer, *Look to the Rock* (IVP, 1996), pp. 157–161.

8 Why does the NIV reduce this dramatic statement to 'even to the end'?

Psalm 125

## 8 Keeping on keeping on: The encircling Lord

It's always the best and safest course to assume that the Lord knows what he is doing, though it is not necessarily the easiest line to take! Isaiah pointed us in the right direction. Thinking of the calamitous history of his people and foreseeing the tribulations of defeat and deportation, he did not ask the question 'Why?' but the question 'Who?'

> Who handed Jacob over to become loot,
> and Israel to the plunderers?
> Was it not the Lord . . . ? (Isaiah 42:24)

Ask that question, listen to the answer, and begin to feel safe, no matter what the trial. By-pass the people who are talking about 'Satan getting in' – he can do only what he is directed and allowed to do.[1] Go straight to the top. No one can pluck us out of his hand! That's where we were when trouble struck; that's where we are for all time and eternity. We live in the hand that appoints our experiences and our destiny, and which controls our daily circumstances. This is not a problem; it is a fact; it is also the softest pillow on which to lay our heads. Our God is really and truly God.

## Home, but not yet home

Psalm 125 is the third psalm in its triad, and like all the 'third psalms' in the Songs of the Great Ascent it is a psalm of homecoming. Psalm 123 found us at the end of our tether, under the pressures of a hostile, mocking world (compare Psalm 120); Psalm 124 described the hazards of the pilgrim way (compare Psalm 121), and the Lord's sufficiency. In Psalm 125 we are, at last, as safe as houses, as strong and stable as Mount Zion (verse 1), as secure in the Lord as Jerusalem, itself a hilltop city, and made doubly impregnable by its girdle of encompassing hills (verse 2).

And yet . . . and yet . . . ! How often this must have been the experience of the pilgrims to Zion. They reach the city of their desires, and as a city, in itself (122:3) and in its location (125:2), it is all they ever imagined, but, maybe, its current king is one of the less-than-adequate inheritors of David's throne, or, maybe, their pilgrimage coincides with one of those all-too-numerous occasions when some international threat loomed over the city, or, maybe, following the political astuteness but spiritual lunacy of Ahaz,[2] the throne of David is now but a mere puppet monarchy, and the real sceptre is in foreign, pagan hands. Yes, Zion is still the chosen city, and it is good almost beyond imagining (122:2) to be there, but real peace still eludes, still lies somewhere out there, a hope for the misty future (verse 5b).

This is Psalm 125! This is where it addresses us. It is a yes and no psalm; it reflects exactly where we are. How are we to react to the presence, prevalence and oppressiveness of the 'sceptre' of wickedness'?[3] For as we look around our world this is the lot of believers. The pressures vary, the shoe pinches in different ways and with different degrees of pain, but only the coming of the Lord Jesus will bring all who trust him for their salvation, the Israel of God, into the peace he has for us. Till then, the road winds uphill all the way.

## Question one

In what way, we wonder, was wickedness waving its sceptre over the 'land allotted to the righteous' (verse 3)? Many associate the psalm with Nehemiah 6,[4] but the situation envisaged is wider than any specific application. Even David's reign was not wholly free from evidence of

the 'sceptre of wickedness'; Absalom – not altogether without cause –
blew the trumpet of rebellion, using his hands to do evil, as the psalm
would accuse him. Israelite society was always divided, with (verse 3)
the 'righteous' (those right with God), (verse 4) the 'good' (those
cultivating and evidencing wholesome moral living), and the 'upright in
heart' (people spiritual in character and objectives) on the one side, and
(verse 5) the 'crooked'[5] and deviants ('evildoers')[6] on the other. At any
time when pilgrim feasts were observed – right up to Luke 2:41–52 –
Psalm 125 justified its place in the Pilgrims' Hymnbook, and we pilgrims
today, sheltered by infinitely more precious and potent blood, can still
find ourselves addressed, in teaching and comfort, by its timeless words.
The 'sceptre of wickedness' is always in evidence, sometimes in the
ascendant, constantly in operation: it is the world in which we live.

## Question two

What, then, is the 'evil'[7] to which we can be tempted to put our hands
(verse 3)? For we have all experienced the 'Why should I put up with
this any longer?' moment, and that's the danger point. When patient
endurance runs out, sinfulness comes running in; impatience and
making golden calves have for a long time been a solidly married
couple.[8]

## Divine sovereign rule

Within Psalm 125 there are clear suggestions of the form golden calves
may well take when we weary of dominant wickedness and put our
hands to evil. The first is to rebel against the way the Lord is ruling the
world. The 'sceptre of wickedness' can remain in place only for as long
as he appoints. He is watchful over his people, and will not allow them
to be tested beyond their strength (1 Corinthians 10:12–13). In righteousness he has raised up the current ruler, and when the right and righteous
time comes he will send that ruler packing.[9] That's the way the world
is. That is the secret story behind the public story, and our calling is to
'submit . . . to the governing authorities, for there is no authority except
that which God has established. The authorities that exist have been

established by God . . . he who rebels against the authority is rebelling against what God has instituted'.[10] So much of the history of the kings of Israel and Judah stands as proof of the seriousness and veracity of this biblical world view. The fantastically silly Zedekiah was king while Jeremiah was counselling submission to the 'sceptre of wickedness' in the shape of Babylon (see endnote 4). Jeremiah's way would have preserved Jerusalem intact, its people still in residence, its house of the Lord undamaged and functioning; Zedekiah's rebellion saw the people trailing off as exiles to Babylon, the house of God despoiled and demolished, and the city a smoking ruin. The Bible would say to us, would it not, 'Take your pick!'?

### Giving God a helping hand

Psalm 125:1 and 2 sound the note of absolute security. In verse 1 Zion's true citizens, those who are trusting in the Lord, are as secure as the city itself is secure, because of the (hilltop) position in which it is placed and because of the elect status it enjoys as the 'place the Lord has chosen'.[11] In verse 2, the city is secure, protected, geographically and militarily speaking, by its girdle of hills, but, much more, with the actually impregnable shield of the surrounding Lord.[12] When, however, the 'sceptre of wickedness' loomed – the Assyrian threat – King Ahaz' first thought was for his water supply (Isaiah 7:3). Being Ahaz, he might well have been saying in his heart, 'What an absurd city for the Lord to choose: one with only an overland supply of water that any and every invader can cut off!' What Ahaz probably thought, Hezekiah remedied (2 Kings 20:20). His tunnel was a technological marvel, as well as a masterstroke of civil amenity and military foresight. Now the kings of Jerusalem could laugh in the face of any 'sceptre of wickedness': 'Yah, boo! You'll never dry us out! We've got our tunnel!' Do you see now why Isaiah thought Hezekiah's tunnel was the unforgivable sin?[13] It put to rights what the Lord had got wrong. It implicitly accused the Lord of foolishness and thoughtlessness. It acted on the assumption that the Lord didn't know what he was doing, and needed human wisdom to get things right. It gave poor old God a helping hand! It affirmed that salvation lay in technology – human 'know-how-can-do'.[14] It replaced faith by works.

It always pays to assume that the Lord knows what he is doing, and to wait trustfully for him.

## Facing life

When trials come, then, and unwelcome forces are dominant, we have the negative task of restraining our hands from 'doing evil', certainly refusing salvation by either force or works. Is there a corresponding positive course? Yes, there is, and it can be simply stated.

First, we must renew our confidence in the actual and total security that is ours by divine appointment. We are as fixed and immoveable as Mount Zion itself (verse 1) and we are just as amply protected (verse 2). See how each verse says 'for ever'. The position we have, simply as believers (verse 1a), is as 'given' as the realities of creation, as immoveable as a mountain (verse 1), and as guaranteed as divine faithfulness (verse 2). Or, to put it in the words of the Lord Jesus Christ, we are in his hand, and nothing and no one can shift us (John 10:28, 29). No danger can alter our security. The trouble is, however, that we can forget how secure we are, and where our security lies. It is, therefore, our first port of call when trouble looms; it is our first task to look our trouble in the face and affirm 'I believe in God the Father Almighty'.

Our second port of call is the place of prayer. Look at the shape of the psalm:

A$^1$ (vv. 1–2) Our security in the Lord: the way of faith
   B (v. 3) A dangerous world: the sceptre of wickedness
A$^2$ (vv. 4–5) Our resource in the Lord: the way of prayer

See how the threats and pressures of experience (B) are bracketed by our security (A$^1$) and our prayers (A$^2$). Keep that picture in mind. This is the way to handle life.

Remarkably, the suggested prayers are only indirectly (if at all) concerned with changing the circumstances that prompted them. The 'sceptre of wickedness' is still in place. The temptation to turn to evil is still as pressing. The prayers of the saints are concerned exclusively with moral issues: that in the world as it is – 'sceptre of wickedness' and all – those who are right with God may experience his loving care (verse 4), and those who are otherwise come under his judgment (verse 5). We should not be afraid to model our praying, in our present world, on this pattern. In essence, like all prayers, this is a 'leave it to the Lord' exercise,[15] but when we pray about moral and spiritual issues, and ask for moral and spiritual consequences, we know that we pray according to his will – both for blessing (verse 4) and for banishment (verse 5).

To put it another way: in the thick of difficult experiences, whatever form the 'sceptre of wickedness' may take – an oppressive, persecuting regime, a difficult, unpredictable superior, an uncongenial circumstance – we must look beyond it in our prayers, and pray for the coming divine settlement of all things, when at last the Lord's Israel (verse 5b), you and me and all who trust in Jesus as Saviour, will enter into perfect peace: the full reality of peace with God, the peace of perfect fellowship among perfected saints, and the peace of our characters at last fully fashioned in the likeness of Christ.

---

## Notes

1 Job 1:8, 12; 2:2, 6.

2 2 Kings 16; 2 Chronicles 28:16–25; Isaiah 7, See Motyer, *The Prophecy of Isaiah* (IVP, 1993), pp. 80–88; *Isaiah*, IVP, TOTC, 1999, pp. 74–78.

3 This is what the Hebrew says in verse 3. The NIV prefers to alter the vowels of the Masoretic Text.

4 E.g. Wilcock and Allen point broadly to post-exilic enemy occupation. We need to be careful not to confuse suitability with origin. Many 'matches' can be drawn between the psalm and Nehemiah's Jerusalem, but this does not have the consequence that the psalm was composed then. The implications of the psalm were true all through Zion's troubled history.

5 Literally, 'who turn aside / misdirect their crooked ways', i.e. a double charge, their ways are crooked and they themselves are intent on going in the wrong direction.

6 In verse 5 NIV 'evildoers' represents *'po'aley – 'awen*, practitioners of *'awen*; *'awen* is a versatile word. On twenty-eight occasions it is an undefined, general mark of the wicked – maybe of speech (Psalm 10:7) or of conduct (Psalm 28:3). In twenty-six cases it has the broad meaning of trouble or mischief. In Psalm 6, 'you who do evil' could simply mean 'mischief-makers'; compare 14:4. Eighteen times it means 'that which

troubles God' or 'causes his displeasure', e.g. 92:9 <10>. There are five examples of its use with cultic, religious associations (e.g. Isaiah 1:13, NKJV 'iniquity'; NIV 'evil') and eight examples connected with false worship (e.g. Isaiah 66:3, 'idol'). Generally speaking the idea is 'wrong', usually if not always with the related idea of the trouble that that wrong brings. A wide significance suits Psalm 125:5, 'wrongdoers', without specifying what.

7 The noun *awelah* means 'deviancy', 'departure from the norm'. Here it is in the extended feminine form, for emphasis, *awelathah*.

8 Exodus 32:1–6.

9 Compare Isaiah 10:5–15; Jeremiah 25:8–12; 27:6.

10 Romans 13:1, 2; compare Daniel 2:21; 4:17; 25, 32; 5:21.

11 Deuteronomy 12:4, 10–12; 1 Kings 8:17–22; Psalm 132:13, 14.

12 Compare Isaiah 33:20–22; Zechariah 2:5.

13 Isaiah 22:8b–11, 14.

14 Compare Genesis 11:1–9.

15 Compare Romans 12:19.

Psalms 126 – 131

# 9  A preview: The pilgrimage of the heart

It's like stepping into a different world when we come to Psalms 126 – 128 and 129 – 131.

By now we are familiar with the thought that the Songs of the Great Ascent fall into triads, groups of three. So far, the first of each three is a psalm of lament over the harshness of living in this world: how uncongenial (120), and contemptuous (123) it is! The second in each group is a psalm of divine sufficiency: the keeping Lord (121), competent for every threat (124); and the third, a psalm of homecoming: joy (122) and security (125) in Zion.

The triad beginning with Psalm 126 is the same – but different! The first two triads end in Zion (122:2; 125:1–2). This third triad starts there (126:1). Psalm 127 does not mention Zion by name, but it is a 'city' psalm, raising the question of what makes a city secure (1), and what might happen if the gate were under threat from enemies (5); in Psalm 128, Zion is the centre of divine blessing (5). The whole series of three lies inside a 'Zion' bracket (126:1; 128:5). The picture and motifs of pilgrimage *to* Zion have been replaced by matters to do with life *within* Zion, but not yet a perfect Zion experience. In 126, the outside world is still there, but now watching in admiration (verse 2), not in hostility or contemptuousness; 127 raises serious problems: house-building, guarding the city, anxious nights and early rising (verses 1–2), and the problem of hostile attack (verse 5). Yet, as in Psalms 121 and 124, Psalm 127 has a strong sense that the Lord is the answer to all these situations. He is the house-builder, the watchman on the walls, and the generous giver of a strong family. And, like Psalms 122 and 125, Psalm 128 records the enjoyment of blessing: blessing for every faithful one (verse 1), blessing in marriage and family (verses 2–4), Zion-centred blessing reaching to future generations (verses 5–6) – a psalm not of homecoming but of being at home.

The same, but different. The pilgrim path now lies in the heart of the pilgrim, not longing now for a far-off city, but, as within Zion, longing for greater and renewed blessing (126); facing the problems of life and still promised divine sufficiency (127), and (128) at last under the desired blessing, personally, domestically and perpetually (128). It is the pilgrimage of the heart: the longing to know afresh and in abundant measure the blessings of the past (126); the longing to learn more perfectly to trust the Lord in the pressing anxieties of each day, and to trust him to provide in advance for problems that may yet arise (127); the longing for final perfection, the full reality of what the Bible means by 'peace': the well-being of a heart without inner tensions or warring desires; peace in a perfected fellowship, and peace with God. It is what Psalm 128 envisages in its own terms; it is where the heart of the pilgrim longs to be.

## Zion, past, present and future

All this matches – and is perfectly illustrated by – the way the Bible thinks of Zion or Jerusalem. There is David's Jerusalem; there is its 'development' or 'fulfilment' (Matthew 5:17), the Jerusalem of which every believer in Jesus is a citizen,[1] and there is the perfection of Jerusalem, the Lamb's wife, yet to come down from God out of heaven, the summation of the New Earth.[2] It's like what gardeners call a 'perennial'. It flowers every year, but its first flowering, while it is a true flowering, falls far short of its coming maturity. So it is that David's Jerusalem is not put at a discount or negligible. Rather it is the first flowering. The final flowering, when it comes, will be the eternal maturing of everything that was present in principle and intended from the start.

Meanwhile, we are betwixt and between. In Christ we live in Zion, but we also long for Zion. Zion is ours, yet Zion eludes us. It is in this way that Psalms 126 – 128 speak to our hearts; they address our stage of the pilgrimage. And the same applies to the next triad, Psalms 129 – 131. In Psalm 129 Israel – the Jesus people[3] – and Zion – their location – are both under attack. Suffering is intense, but there is no question where victory lies. The world consists of two groups in tension, but only one is under divine blessing. Yet that one group, Israel, the Jesus people, the inhabitants of Zion, groan under conviction of sin (130:1–2) and acknowledge its seriousness before God (130:3), but at the same time they know his forgiveness (130:4) and his unfailing love, and look for coming full redemption (130:7–8). For this they wait with agonized longing (130:5), but (Psalm 131) they are at rest in the Lord, and enjoy confident hope.

This, again, is our 'in-between' state. We have arrived in Zion; we are its assured citizens, tasting its joys, but at the same time not yet in the Zion that, some glad day, Zion will assuredly be. For this we long, while, as things are, as Zion's citizens, we also live in 'this vale of tears'.

---

### Notes

1 Galatians 4:21–28; Hebrews 12:22–24.

2 Revelation 21:9 – 22:5.

3 Compare Romans 9:6–8; Galatians 4:28; 6:16; etc.

Psalm 126

10 Instant coffee and stalactites: Living
with God's tensions

Psalm 126 has a message of great practical importance for us. If we
think of a pilgrimage on foot, the vital thing is taking the next
step . . . and the next . . . and the next . . . and then the next. However
loved and desired the goal, it will never be reached without that next
step!

The matching truth for a pilgrimage of the heart is setting true and
realistic goals, and planning stage by stage how to get there. The goal
is our *vision*; the next step is our *policy*. Keep this distinction in mind.
Someone once said, 'Ask a Christian minister lately arrived at a new
charge, "What's your policy?" and often the reply will be, "To see this
church full, without an empty seat." No, that's not a policy; that's a
vision. A policy is how you are going to get there!'[1] Visions are great
and indispensable. We must, indeed, be careful to make them as great,
glorious, lofty and clear as the Bible allows. But our policy must always
be kept severely within the bounds of what is practical, realistic and
manageable. Otherwise the vital 'next step' is not defined, and will never
be taken.

## Satan, the idealist

For example, do you remember the last time you started to draw up a daily prayer list? Names of people needing our prayers come flooding into mind. It was suddenly essential to pray for dear X labouring so valiantly in Y, and she proved to be only one of a countless number who hitherto had managed very well without my prayers but who suddenly must now find a place on my list. And before we know where we are, the prayer list has reached proportions quite beyond what time, energy and ability can manage. In other words, the *vision* is magnificent, but the *policy* has got out of hand. And Satan chuckles and chalks up another victory. He has so enlarged our vision that in fact there is no possibility of taking the next step!

Or here is something dear to the heart of every believer. Something truly essential; the vision of all visions: to be like Jesus. 'Right,' says Satan, 'Start by being holy as he is holy.' In other words, replace one colossal vision by another – and put the matter beyond our reach. Rather, why not try bringing the 'vision' into the sphere of 'policy'? Let's face it: we will never be like Jesus in holiness until he comes again and 'we shall be like him, for we shall see him' (1 John 3:2), but I can (for example) set myself to know the Bible as he knew it; I can plan a manageable, realistic programme of daily Bible reading; I can set myself to memorize a verse a week – or whatever. I can progressively build up my knowledge of the word of God. I can step out on to the pilgrim road by planning the next step . . . and the next . . . and the next. Satan does not mind how idealistic we are, provided the ideals remain unrealizable. He hates policies, and the more practical they are, the greater the hate! He can defeat us with visions; we can defeat him with policies.

## Past and present

Psalm 126 calls visionaries to order: don't ever allow your vision to become dim, but, please, work out a practical policy for each day – your own pilgrimage of heart and foot!

There are important truths in every part of this psalm, and some of them we can note only in passing, but if we start by allowing the psalm to fall into its clear divisions its main thrust will, I hope, emerge. First, the thought of 'bringing back captives' links verses 1 and 4;[2] note also how the 'we were' of verse 1 finds a small echo in the 'we are' of verse 3. The mighty work of the Lord (verse 1a), done without human co-operation or contribution (we were in dreamland at the time, verse 1b), leads to vocal responses: first the recipients of the benefit of the mighty work open their 'mouths' and use their 'tongues' in 'laughter' and 'joy' (verse 2a), and then we hear the voice of the watching world noting the 'great things' the Lord has done for his people (verse 2b). Following verses 3–4, in which another 'we' rejoices in what the Lord has done, and asks for more of the same, an unidentified voice speaks (verses 5–6) about 'songs of joy' arising out of the laborious work of sowing (verses 5a, 6a), and the fruitful work of reaping (verses 5b, 6b).[3]

$A^1$ (v. 1) Restoration
    a The work of the Lord
    b His sole work, without human contribution
  $B^1$ (v. 2) Voices in response
      a The vocal joy of the recipients
      b The observing world
$A^2$ (vv. 3–4) Restoration
        a Joy in what the Lord has done (v. 3)
        b Prayer for more of the same (v. 4)
  $B^2$ (vv. 5–6) Another voice: A promise doubled
        a Tears and joy, sowing and reaping
        b Weeping and joy, seed and sheaves

There, in review, is the situation we must explore. How does the past relate to the present? In the past lies a great work of God, which he did for us without us. Is this the model on which we are to plan the present? Do we continue in a dreamlike spectator state, leaving it all to him? And if not, then what?

## Miracle and providence

The translation of the key words in verses 1 and 4 remains uncertain. Is it a broad thought like 'restoring fortunes', or does it refer, more specifically, to 'bringing back captivity'? In the most basic sense it really doesn't matter! The important thing is not to try to be too specific. For example, any reference to 'captives' or 'captivity' can lead all too easily to making a link between the psalm and the end of the Babylonian Captivity in 539 BC, and the return of a smallish but very heroic band to homeland and city.[4] The psalm does fit in with that period of history, just as also it fits in with the later time of Nehemiah,[5] but it would be equally at home, say, with Sennacherib's invasion in 705 BC and the great deliverance recorded in 2 Kings 19:35, 36. And the same applies to any and every experience of duress that came to Zion, whether by foreign invasion or on account of the rotten government of many an inadequate Davidic king. Indeed, Psalm 126 could even be a meditation on the fundamental reversal of fortunes and bringing back of captives in and at the exodus itself – not that 'Zion' existed in exodus times, but that a later poet could thoughtfully use the name proleptically,[6] describing an earlier situation in terms of the later reality: everything the Lord ever did was for those who were destined to be his 'Zion people'.

Many signal divine deliverances, restorations and fresh starts marked the history of the Lord's people. Many a time he sidelined them – as he did with Adam in Genesis 2:21, or with Abram in Genesis 15:12[7] – and by his own sole operation and volition accomplished their salvation. At the Red Sea they 'stood still' (NKJV) and watched 'the salvation of the Lord' (Exodus 14:13). Was it from that moment that they knew the Lord their God as the one who, without any action by or contribution from them, was their Saviour? Did they find themselves standing on the other side of the Red Sea 'like men who dreamed', waking to find the Lord had done everything on their behalf?

So it is with our salvation in Christ. The Old Testament would be happy to define the God it reveals as 'the Lord who came down to Egypt to save his people', but, stepping from Malachi to Matthew, we find nothing has changed. He is still 'the Lord who comes down to save' – this time, through birth of a virgin, in the person of him who is 'Immanuel, God with us', and whose name is Jesus because 'it is he that shall save his people from their sins' (RV). The task is all his, the benefit all ours. He, the giver, we, the recipients! As to Jesus in his saving death, we can only be onlookers and reporters, while sharing in the glory to be revealed (1 Peter 5:1). This is the wonder and the non-negotiable heart of the biblical message of salvation. In Paul's dramatic summary, balancing the negative with the positive:

Not because of righteous things we had done,
but because of his mercy,
he saved us.[8]


## Praying for more

Our parallel with Psalm 126 does not end there. With the people of
the psalm we too look back at a (in our case 'the') great divine act
of salvation (verse 1a). We too slept the sleep of the designedly inactive
while the Lord did it all (verse 1b); we too sing out our responsive
joy, for in the Bible singing symbolizes our entrance with joy into a
salvation to which we have made no contribution;[9] and we too can
re-echo the prayer of verse 4, whether it be translated 'restore our
fortunes' or 'bring back our captivity'. For, like our brothers and sisters
of old, we are both enjoying a salvation already achieved and awaiting
a salvation yet to come. The saving divine Lord Jesus who came down
into our Egypt at his first advent will come down to Egypt yet again
at his second coming, and we who have already been saved, and progressively are being saved, will then experience our consummated
salvation.[10] It is for this we long, and, while we 'groan inwardly as we
wait eagerly for our adoption' (Romans 8:23) it is for this we pray, the
ultimate coming of God our Saviour to our Egypt, to finalize our
eternal bliss.

The suddenness and factual reality of the second coming finds an
apt illustration in 'like streams in the Negev' (Psalm 126:4b). Here is a
riverbed baked dry in the blistering heat of summer,[11] but, far away
in the hills, rain has poured down, the hillside rivulets become cascades,
the waters gathered force, and suddenly the dry channel is a foaming,
roaring, dancing torrent. Instantaneous transformation! Who wouldn't
want it, long for it, pray for it – a transforming work of God in a single,
divine act which changes all, solves all, does all!


## Waiting for miracle, living with providence

And it will happen, just like that, as the Bible says 'in a flash, in the
twinkling of an eye, at the last trumpet' (1 Corinthians 15:52), but, in

the meantime, the psalm has a word of great wisdom to share with us as we hear the unidentified voice speak in verses 5–6.[12] The God of miracles, doing his unaided wonders on our behalf, becomes the God of providence, setting our lives within the ordered workings of Creation as he has ordained it. Prayer for the suddenness of sole divine action is answered by a voice directing the steady, demanding work of sowing seed and waiting patiently for harvest.

This is a really important truth, and we may put it like this: pray to the God of miracles; walk through your pilgrim day with the God of providences. If you are ill, pray for healing, and go immediately to the doctor. Oh, yes, indeed, God heals today, but, for the most part, he does it through the medical sciences he has graciously brought into being. You have a headache? Ask God to soothe it away, and then take an aspirin, for the humble aspirin is his providential provision for that situation. Every harvest of every kind comes only by the gift of God, but it comes through the dedicated (and often costly) obedience of his people to the rules of sowing and reaping which he has built into his creation.

Take the Hebrew words of verse 5 exactly as they stand:

They who sow
with tears
with loud shouts
will reap.

Here is the whole of life stated in one succinct principle: we long for the transition from tears to joy (or, as verse 4 pictures it, from drought to abundant waters); the journey from the one to the other is the long pathway from sowing to reaping. That's life!

Verse 6 broadens the truth out, insisting that no one is exempt, that every capacity for persistence, even endurance, must be called into play, but that the outcome is guaranteed and unstinting. The contrast between sorrow and joy is repeated, but there is also the contrast between the single seeds planted and the sheaves carried home:

Whoever determines to go
even with weeping,
    carrying the line of seed,[13]

    will certainly come
      with loud shouts,
        carrying his sheaves.

## Instant coffee and stalactites

You see now the point of the title given to this psalm. The Lord's instant coffee is the best, rich in taste and aroma, satisfying, creating an appetite for more of the same (verse 4), and focusing the attention of the watching world in wonder and awe (verse 2b).[14] But there is also a different divine work, 'deep in unfathomable mines of never-failing skill, he treasures up his bright designs and works his sovereign will',[15] as, drip by slow drip, the stalactite reaches down from the ceiling of the cave and the stalagmite grows up from the floor, until, in the course of millennia, a pillar of matchless beauty is created. So it is with the providential ordering of God. No harvest without sowing. That is for certain! If, in the interim, the sower is spared tears and weeping, that is a bonus of grace, yet, one way or another, as Jesus taught, the seed never goes unchallenged, nor do those who receive it go untested (e.g. Mark 4:1–20). The toiling farmer, says Paul, must be the first to enjoy the crop (2 Timothy 2:6); the patient farmer, says James, awaits the autumn and spring rains with steady endurance, looking forward to the precious crop (James 5:7–8). These are our pilgrim models.

## Notes

1 A lecturer whose name I have forgotten at a conference for ministers at Pine Mountain, Georgia, USA in 1969. Many apologies to a very helpful and perceptive speaker who deserves better!
2 The NIV, unforgivably, obscures this. Whether the Hebrew is understood as 'bringing back captives' (e.g. RV, NASB, NKJV) or 'restoring fortunes' (e.g. NRSV, ESV), the translation of verses 1 and 4 should be identical, as the Hebrew requires, otherwise how can English readers engage in serious Bible study?
3 Maybe we should think of verses 1–4 as the 'original' psalm – the psalm as the author intended it to be sung. It would form a beautifully and artistically balanced poem with two 'bring back' statements as brackets,

with two responses 'Then . . . then' (verse 2) inside. But when the psalm was sung publicly, a prophetic voice 'intruded' with a word of direction from the Lord. For an example of this, see how the oracle of Jahaziel responded to the prayer of Jehoshaphat, 2 Chronicles 20:5–13, 14–17.

4 Ezra 1 – 3.

5 See Wilcock, p. 232.

6 Just as, e.g. we might say 'the Prime Minister/President was born on . . . ', meaning a baby was born on that date who would one day become prime minister/president.

7 Compare 2 Kings 19:35, 'when the people got up the next morning' – while they slept the Lord had dealt completely with their need of salvation.

8 Titus 3:4, 5.

9 E.g. Exodus 15:1; Psalms 40:1–3; 96:1, 2; 98:1; Isaiah 54:1.

10 E.g. 'you have been saved' (Ephesians 2:8); the message of the cross is the power of God 'to us who are being saved' (1 Corinthians 1:18); and having been reconciled to God through the death of his Son, 'we shall be saved' (Romans 5:10; compare Romans 13:11; Hebrews 9:28).

11 The 'Negev' is the desert land extending from the south of Judah down into the Sinai Peninsula. See *New Bible Dictionary 3rd Edition* (IVP, 1996) under Negev, Palestine.

12 See Outline, p. 75 above.

13 'The line of seed' is an abbreviated way of saying 'enough seed to sow right along the line of the furrow'.

14 Compare Joshua 2:8–11; 1 Samuel 4:5–8; 1 Kings 17:23, 24.

15 W. Cowper's hymn, 'God moves in a mysterious way his wonders to perform'.

Psalm 127

## 11 Managing life's cares: Busyness and restfulness

There are enough anxiety-creating topics in Psalm 127 to make anyone go grey in a night! Building a house (verse 1a) with all the hassle of architects, plans, planning applications, builders, dust, dirt, rubble, delays in materials; not to speak of the money side: the bills pouring in, the mortgage to be paid off. And as if that wasn't pressure enough, here comes the community charge: someone has to pay for the police to keep the city secure (verse 1b), as well as other proper safeguards such as street lighting and rubbish collection. Then (verse 3) the children are growing up, and babyhood costs become, for many, school fees, or, if not that, horrendous expenses for sports kits, musical instruments and lessons, camps and keeping up with the teenage Joneses – the list is endless!

**Perils of the heart**

Yes, indeed, facing life means facing demands, pressures and worries: mortgage, rates and education. It's not all fun being an adult, and it's all there in Psalm 127. Psalm 126 called us to the hard graft of sowing and reaping and the disciplined endurance needed to keep going. The emphasis in Psalm 127 is not, however, on the effort needed for life's tasks, but on the worries accompanying them that mount up and oppress, and could so easily wear us down. Nothing unusual or out of the way . . . the ordinary, inescapable worries that go along with ordinary, average obligations! In a word, Psalm 127 is a typical second psalm in its group. The hazards of the pilgrim path (121), and its typical hostilities (124), are replaced by the constant pressures that would stop the pilgrim heart in its tracks, but if (as is the case) the Lord is powerful against outward assaults (as those psalms insist), he is also sufficient against inward dangers. It is the task of Psalm 127 to reveal this sufficiency.

### What's your problem?

There are two words in particular that bring the problem Psalm 127 faces into sharp focus. Superficially, there seems to be a contrast between making an effort and leaving it to the Lord. In verse 1a we meet a chap building his house but getting nowhere, apparently, because it is all self-effort, whereas he would be better advised to step aside in favour of divine action; in verse 1b, the local community bobby is on his rounds, but, likewise, achieving nothing, so why not leave that to the Lord as well?

Did you never meet up with a preacher calling on his hearers to 'let go and let God'? If not, you have lived a blessedly sheltered life! But it sounds so right, doesn't it? After all, we are saved by faith, not by works, and, over and over, the Bible calls us to live by faith, so is it not obvious that we should throw effort aside and leave all to the Lord? Many have preached exactly that, especially in connection with our personal sanctification, and our longing for some, supposed 'higher life' – some state of spiritual exaltation where enjoyment rules, and no further effort is required! Heaven on earth!

Please don't believe it! Psalm 127 offers, in a nutshell, the perspective the whole Bible shares. And so we come to the two key words.

** The first is translated (three times) 'in vain' (verses 1–2), and is the Hebrew word *shaw'*. The easiest way to understand what this word means is to compare it with another word, *hebhel*, likewise usually translated 'in vain' or 'vanity', as in Ecclesiastes 1:2 (NKJV): 'all is vanity' (NIV 'meaningless'). As used in this way, *hebhel* means 'baffling'. The way things happen to us, and in the world at large, is 'baffling'; things just 'don't add up'. If Psalm 127 had used *hebhel* of house-building, it would mean that the builder is doing his best and *getting nowhere* at speed, baffled and frustrated at every turn by the unexpected, the inexplicable and the insurmountable. By comparison, *shaw'* means 'nothing/nothingness'. In this case the house gets built but *achieves nothing*, has no intrinsic worth. All the labour and expenditure, all the fighting against odds, did result in a house, but not in an achievement of worth. It turned out to be a 'nothing'.

** The second word is translated 'toiling' (verse 2). It is the word *"tsabbim*, which means 'pains',[1] and it is this underlying sense of burdensomeness that runs right through the whole sequence of nouns arising from the verb. That has led the ESV to offer the translation 'anxious toil', or the Book of Common Prayer to render it as 'carefulness' (where we should note specially the first syllable!). It was from this sort of nerve-racking anxiety in a busy life that the Lord Jesus wished to rescue Martha (Luke 10:41), and for which Paul offered the antidote of prayer (Philippians 4:6).[2]

### Why pray when you can worry?

If you looked up the reference to Luke 10:41 (which, of course, you did), you will have come away with a clear picture, contrasting the tearing anxiousness of someone running everywhere and getting nowhere, and the calmness and quiet restfulness of sitting at Jesus' feet. And that brings us back to our psalm. When we read it with really attentive eyes we note the build-up to the end of verse 2: 'labour' (verse 1a), early rising (verse 1b), hurrying to get out of bed and delaying to get back to bed (verse 2a), the 'working breakfast', lunch and supper turned into business meetings – (verse 2b) 'the bread of pain and grief',[3] . . . (verse 2b) 'sleep'!

Some choose to understand the noun 'sleep' as adverbial, 'in sleep' / while they sleep'. This is perfectly permissible. It makes us look back to Psalm 126. Did not the Lord accomplish his work of salvation without our co-operation, while we were in dreamland (126:1), and should there not be something of this principle running through all our life? A realization that not only in salvation is the Lord the Doer, but in every department and aspect of life? A clear grasp of the fact that when, in eternity, we sing 'Glory be to the Father, and to the Son, and to the Holy Spirit' we are actually affirming precisely that as the total explanation and causation of how we sinners received salvation, threaded and fought our way through the dangers and vicissitudes of life and passed through death into Jesus' presence – not at any point did we contribute anything. It was all of God, all of grace.

Others prefer the plainer understanding that sleep is itself his gift. There is a place for resting, for withdrawing, for putting the conflict on one side, putting the feet up, and this, too, is God's grace at work. His providential order is daylight for work, night for sleep (Psalm 104:19–23), six days for work, one day for rest; his plan is also that even in the moments of intensest and most demanding activity our hearts should continue resting in him.

The rendering 'in sleep' points to the Lord as the ceaseless worker on our behalf. He never stops. He 'will neither slumber nor sleep' (Psalm 121:4). He does not fashion his timetable to match ours. Our welfare, plans, longings, ambitions, projects, needs, career advancement – whatever – can be safely left with him. He is 'the giving God' ( James 1:5); it is his good pleasure to give us the kingdom (Luke 12:32); 'he who began a good work in you will carry it on to completion[4] until the day of Christ' (Philippians 1:6). The other understanding, that he 'gives sleep', underlines his gentle care for us. He knows when we have 'had enough'. Night-time reflects his perfect ordering of things, and those who know that they and all their affairs and their loved ones are in the hands of a totally and gloriously sovereign God lay their heads on that truth as on the softest pillow, and await the divine hand that closes their eyes.

## Solomon?

It is fashionable among commentators to dismiss the ascription of Psalm 127 to Solomon as a later editorial addition. The more thoughtful of them go on to point to features in the psalm that may have led such an editor to think of Solomon. They do not, however, often ask the question; if there are these evidences of suitability, why discount Solomon's authorship?[5] But why indeed? The psalm can be seen to offer a perceptive sidelight on Solomon's thinking as he mounted David's throne. What, we might wonder, made him ask the Lord for wisdom (1 Kings 3:9) if he did not (as indeed he indicates) deeply doubt his ability to handle the royal responsibilities now his – as a matter of fact, responsibilities for building, the guardianship of city and kingdom, and, no doubt, knowing Solomon, already a steadily growing brood of sons? The Book of Kings depicts him as assured, master of his life, sometimes all too decisive in decision-making, but, underneath the façade, he was the same common clay as the rest of us. And the Lord took him at the level of his actual nature and need. He gave to 'his beloved one' (verse 2)[6] – to Solomon whom the Lord named 'Jedidiah', the beloved of the Lord (2 Samuel 12:24, 25) – all he asked and needed while he was in dreamland (1 Kings 3:5).

### Disease and antidote

Assuming, then, that Solomon composed this psalm, and that he did so as a candid meditation on the situation he found himself in, he saw ahead a pathway of endless duties, ceaseless activities, working – as people would say today – twenty-four-seven, and, at the end of it, what? Would he too become a 'toothless tiger' like his father, a pawn in internal palace squabbles (1 Kings 1)? Would he too hand on unfinished business of dubious morality (1 Kings 2:1–12) to his successor? Maybe, like David, with a divided family which his own failures made him disqualified and unable to rule? With much done, yet little accomplished? And where did it all go wrong in David's case? Why, when 'the thing David had done displeased the Lord' (2 Samuel 11:27).

So, then, was there another possible pathway ahead, one where at every point the Lord was the builder, not man; the Lord was the wall of defence around the city,[7] and the gracious giver of a stalwart family united around their father (verses 3, 5)? Let the Lord be in charge, seen and sought as the 'real' agent in every situation, and sleep well!

### For instance

The balance that the Bible displays is always striking. In our logic the opposite of rest is work or activity. Not so, says Psalm 127; the opposite of rest is restlessness. Oh yes, there is a life of unceasing, grinding 'taking pains', going nowhere. Yet, on the other hand, looking to the future, houses are not built without effort, are they, nor, conserving the past, are cities ever guarded without diligent guards?

So where does the perfect balance lie between burdensome, anxious work and leaving it to the Lord? It is to answer this question that the psalm turns in verses 3–5. At the beginning of verse 3 (in the Hebrew) comes the irretrievably old-fashioned word, 'behold'.[8] It is an important word, though, and should not be overlooked by translators, because it is there for an important purpose: to call attention to something the Bible wants us not to miss. It always says, 'Look at this!', or, in the present case, 'Look at it this way', which turns out to be an invitation to think about the family – its origin (verse 3), the strength (verses 4–5a) and status (verse 5b)[9] it confers – all to be seen as an illustration of what verses 1–2 have been saying. A very telling illustration too!

### The divine gift of a child

If we are to grasp what verses 3–5 are saying, we must start by reminding ourselves of what the Bible teaches about conceiving a baby. We can start with Genesis 29 and 30 where the experience of the two sisters, Leah and Rachel, rings so true. Of course, we are not given dates, but the impression is that Leah conceived on her honeymoon, whereas Rachel, Jacob's other and favourite wife, remained, for some significant length of time, childless. What is important is the way the Bible explains this disparity. The Lord opened Leah's womb (Genesis 29:31), whereas, when the frustrated Rachel expostulated with Jacob, he replied, 'Am I in the place of God, who has kept you from having children?' (30:2).[10] In other words, the Creator has put at our disposal a scheme of cause and effect – sexual intercourse leads to conception – but has retained the effectiveness of that scheme in his own hands.

It is in this sense that 'sons are a heritage from the Lord, children a reward from him.' We – in this case more than happily and enthusiastically – act in conformity with the providential order the Lord has created, but it is for him to accord to us what he thinks we should inherit from him, and what 'reward' or 'return' his grace should confer. This is the picture we are intended to keep in mind, for it is in accordance with this illustration that we are to understand what the psalm is teaching.[11]

We live our whole lives within the ordinances and rules of the Creation. Everything depends on the place we accord to the Creator. As he has organized the world and ordained our place in it, it is our responsibility to provide for home and city, to build and guard, to conform to what has been called the 'creation ordinance' of daily work – but to do so with our eyes constantly fixed on the Creator, to obey his directive of six days' work, one day's rest, to rely on him at every turn of every day's duties, to look to him for the outcome, to understand that prospering is not, in essence, the consequence of skill, commitment and application (however admirable and essential these are) but of blessing divinely bestowed. We 'watch as if on that alone hung the issue of the day'; we 'pray that help may be sent down'; our calling is to 'watch and pray'[12] – or, as an American friend counselled, 'Trust the Lord – and look out for trucks!'

As befits its place as the second psalm in its group, Psalm 127 raises and faces the dangers awaiting us on pilgrimage, here the pilgrimage of our hearts. The danger is the 'I can cope' syndrome, the 'leave it to me' mindset. That way lie all the ineffectiveness, exhaustion, nervous strain, anxiety and potential breakdown against which verses 1–2 warn. Our calling, however, is not to 'obedience' as such, but to 'the obedience of faith'. The mere idea of obedience leads to either 'Of course I can' or (just as wrong) 'Of course I can't'. The obedience of faith says 'Of course I can't, but HE can – so I will!' That is the message of Psalm 127.

---

## Notes

1   The verb, √'atsabh, in all its forms always has a meaning in the range pain, grieve, hurt. The noun, etsebh, refers (Genesis 3:16) to the pains of childbirth, in Proverbs 5:10 to possessions gained by costly effort – by taking pains; 10:22, 'trouble' such as would mar a blessing; 14:23 (see NKJV) contrasts 'work', again 'taking pains' over something with 'mere talk'. Another form of the noun in Isaiah 58:3 suggests 'sweated labour', and another, Psalm 139:24, action that 'pains' the Lord; or, finally, another form in Job 9:28, means 'sufferings'.

2  The noun *merimna* and the verb *merimnao*, 'obsessive worry'.

3  Literally, 'bread of pains', a plural of itemization, 'every sort of pain'.

4  Handley Moule, *Philippian Studies* (Hodder, 1902), 'will evermore put His finishing touches to it'.

5  Solomon is known as an author, particularly of 'songs', and most of all for wisdom expressed in 'proverbs' (1 Kings 4:30–34). This psalm is taken to be a typical 'wisdom' psalm.

6  The literal rendering of what the NIV mistakenly pluralizes into 'those he loves'. The word here is one of the four words the Old Testament uses for 'love'. Often (and well) translated as 'compassion', *rachamim* is love centred and expressed in the emotions, being 'in love' (of the Lord, Psalm 69:16b); *chesedh* is love centred in the will, the love that makes its lifelong commitment in marriage (Psalm 100:5a); *ahabhah* is the love of deep, permanent attachment (Deuteronomy 7:8); and, the word here, *yadhidh*, is beautifully illustrated in Song of Solomon 6:13, the love of the mutual commitment of two lives as one.

7  Compare, Isaiah 26:1; Zechariah 2:5.

8  For that reason omitted in the NIV? See NKJV, ESV.

9  It is not easy to see what exactly verses 4–5 mean by the benefits they see in a large family born to a young parent. We should certainly dismiss anything that savours of 'Touch me if you dare – or I'll send the boys round to have a word with you!' The 'gate' (verse 5) could be either the place from which an attacking force is finally driven (Isaiah 28:6), or the local court for settling disputes (Ruth 4:4; 2 Samuel 15:2): in the former situation, a strong family provides a fighting force; in the latter, a united, mature family group would give status in the community. The reference to 'arrows' (verse 4) is certainly an allusion to strength against any and every opponent. But why 'sons born in one's youth' (verse 4)? Why indeed? Happily, none of these unanswered questions touches the core reason why the family is introduced in the first place.

10  See also Genesis 16:1, 2: Sarai explains her childlessness by saying 'The Lord has kept me from having children'. In 1 Samuel 1:5 the Lord has 'shut' Hannah's womb. Compare Genesis 20:18. Likewise it is God who fashions the embryo in the womb (Job 31:15), times conception to suit what he intends for the child to be born (Jeremiah 1:5), prepares and sets apart the developing fetus for the life and work he has planned (Psalm 139:13–16) etc., etc. Though we cannot follow it through here, all this is of great significance for our attitude to abortion.

11 An obvious related question, for example, is whether couples disappointed regarding conception should seek medical help. In this (as in every matter of health) our first recourse should be to affirm before the Lord our readiness to accept what he wills, and to make our need a matter of prayer, and then, with gratitude, turn to the blessings of medical science which divine providence has provided, still resting on the Lord to give the outcome that he has planned. The question of family planning (subject to using an acceptable method) should rather be linked with the dual purpose the Bible teaches for marital sex – first, that of creating, cementing and maturing the 'one-flesh' relationship, and secondly, as a by-product, procreation.

12 Charlotte Elliott's hymn, 'Christian! seek not yet repose'. *Hymns of Faith*, 375.

Psalm 128

# 12 Home at last: Fulfilment – present, guaranteed and ultimate

The 'fear of the Lord' . . . If we think about it at all, it certainly doesn't figure in our timetable as frequently as the Bible would suggest. Here is a statistic to think about: in one case alone – the verb 'to fear', with its matching noun and adjective[1] – there are at least 170 references to look up!

## Fear that is not fear

When the kingdom of northern Israel fell to the Assyrians, its people were deported to Mesopotamia, and the Assyrian king – known in secular history as Ashurbanipal, but whom the Hebrew, deliciously, calls 'the great and noble Osnappar'[2] – brought a gaggle of foreign importees in to take their place.[3] Experience in their new home gradually brought them to think that perhaps they ought to recognize Yahweh, and we read (2 Kings 17, following NKJV):

** v. 32 'They feared the Lord, and . . . appointed for themselves priests'; i.e. they invented their own religious response.

** v. 33 'They feared the Lord, yet served their own gods.' Their so-called fear did not encroach on the realm of their real loyalty.
** v. 34 'They do not fear the Lord.'[4]

You see? There is a fear that is not a fear. A craven fear, a sheer, numb terror. It issues in man-made ritual – religion without revelation (verse 32); it does not capture the heart or lead to a true devotion (verse 33) – in a word, it is not fear at all (verse 34).

## The genuine article

By way of contrast, the sacred historian, in his careful way, at once introduces the elements of true fear of the Lord:[5]

** v. 35 The true fear of the Lord excludes all recognition of other gods.
** v. 36 The Lord, who redeemed you ('brought you up from the land of Egypt'[6]) is worthy of your 'fear', 'worship' and religious obedience ('sacrifice').
** v. 37 The fear due to him, which excluded fear of other gods, is to be expressed outwardly in obedience to his revealed will.[7]

## What a blessing!

Come now to Psalm 128. It is the third psalm in its group, and is, therefore, as we have learned to expect, a psalm of arrival, with all travails in the past, and all enrichments in the present and expanding into the future. Look at the way this careful poem is shaped:

    A[1] v. 1 A statement in the third person:
        The blessedness of the one who truly fears the Lord
      B[1] (vv. 2–3) Three second-person affirmations: where this
             blessedness is experienced:
               b[1] Personal (v. 2b): the God-fearer himself
               b[2] Marital (v. 3a); his wife
               b[3] Familial (v. 3b): his sons

A² v. 4 A statement in the third person:
　　　Sure blessing for the God-fearer
　B² (vv. 5–6) Three second-person affirmations: where this
　　　　blessing is experienced:
　　　　　　b2¹ Personal (v. 5a): The God-fearer himself
　　　　　　b2² Ecclesial (v. 5b); Jerusalem, the assembled
　　　　　　　Church
　　　　　　b2³ Generational (v. 6); to succeeding
　　　　　　　generations
　　　C v. 6 Summary: Israel at peace[8]

## The fear of the Lord

Each half of the psalm, then, opens with the same theme, the fear of the Lord (verses 1, 4) – not, of course, any sort of bare terror, but, none the less, something that can rightly be called 'fear'. The thought runs through the Bible. Paul speaks of knowing 'what it is to fear the Lord',[9] and of how that fear motivates him to evangelism (2 Corinthians 5:11). He is thinking of his own appearing 'before the judgment seat of Christ' (verse 10), and is plainly moved by the question of whether, though we will be delighted with Jesus, he will be delighted with us. Peter (1 Peter 1:17) calls us to 'live . . . in reverent fear'[10] because we know God as Father, and we know the cost that that Father was prepared to pay for our redemption, namely, 'the precious blood of Christ' (verse 19). In other words, this is a fear that guards us against displeasing One who has so loved and so loves us, coupled with fear lest familiarity with our salvation make us presumptuous.[11]

Maybe we can bring all these sorts of thought into Psalm 128. Surely we can! Nevertheless, the Old Testament has its own testimony to the fear that is due to God. Gideon felt it, and so did Samson's father, but it fell to Isaiah to spell it out, when he said 'Woe is me! I am ruined! For I am a man of unclean lips . . . and my eyes have seen the King, the LORD Almighty.'[12] This is not the (very natural) fear of creature before Creator, but the moral and spiritual fear of a sinner in the presence of the holy God, a fear eternally inseparable from the proper assurance and confidence of status that is ours as sinners saved by grace.

## Evidence

Those who 'fear the Lord' 'walk in his ways' (verse 1). There is a fear that paralyses, reducing us to incoherence and immobility, but there is also a fear that is not fear at all, and it motivates us to holy living.[13] Doubtless it includes Paul's sensitive anticipation of the judgment seat of Christ, which spurred him on to share the gospel with the unsaved. Doubtless also it is close to Peter's longing to live for the good pleasure of such a Saviour and such a Father. But what it actually amounts to is this: the Lord has revealed himself not only in the work of salvation (Exodus 6:6–7) but also in his law, the revealed lifestyle for his redeemed people which matches his holy nature. Those who fear the Lord are the people of revelation in both its aspects: they respond in reverence to the God of their salvation, and, as Psalm 2:11 puts it, they 'rejoice with trembling'; they gladly commit themselves to walking in his ways. As ever, obedience to the word of God is the hallmark of genuineness, the outward evidence of an inner reverence of heart.

## Blessings abound

Psalm 128 uses two words to express the idea of 'blessing', and both follow on from a true fear of the Lord. The fact that the first word (verse 1), in Hebrew *'ashrey*, is often translated 'happy' points us in the right direction. It describes the state or condition of a person – maybe as he or she feels it or as others observe it in them. It is used of someone enjoying divine blessing (e.g. Psalm 1:1); it also expresses contentment or fulfilment in one's life, a meaning which must be included here in Psalm 128, but, in the Bible, the distinction is a fine one, for, certainly in most cases, the state of happy contentment arises from God's favour.[14]

The word in verse 4 is the verb 'to bless', which, used of God's action, means to bestow, by grace and gift, some particular benefit. The change of wording from verse 1 is not accidental. The rewards that follow from fearing the Lord and walking in his ways are not by chance; they are the result of divine action, his chosen benefits. In short, Psalm 128 offers us a pathway of blessedness: the individual concerned[15] finds fulfilment in his work (verse 2a), in his personal life (verse 2b), in his marriage (verse 3a) and in his family (verse 3b).[16] But there is even more.

** v. 4 renews the assurance of blessing, and the psalm goes on to spell out further and fuller benefits flowing from fearing the Lord. In personal life, the earthly blessings of verse 2 are matched, in verse 5a, by lifelong ('all the days') spiritual blessings: for the blessings that flow out of Zion arise from the fact that the Lord lives there, he is present among his people in all his holiness, and they come into his presence through the shed blood of the sacrifices he has appointed. This is what 'Zion' means: his dwelling place, his gift of salvation by grace, through faith, resting on atoning blood.

** The picture of the delightful wife (verse 3a) is now amplified into that of the mother city, Jerusalem in real prosperity, the city mothering its inhabitants as the Lord always intended.[17]

** The sons round the family table in verse 3b are amplified into family life enjoyed in succeeding generations, fulfilling the promise of Exodus 20:6; compare Proverbs 20:7; Acts 2:39.

** There is one final outreaching of this spreading blessing. Before we take note of it, however, remember that everything stems from the God-fearing individual who lives according to God's revealed word. Not only does individual life matter, and not only does the fear of the Lord bring fulfilment to the individual, but the God-fearing individual is the means of blessing in his marriage and family and in the wider family of the city of God, the church, and also the well-being of the whole people of God – 'peace upon Israel' (verse 6) – ultimately rests on his shoulders. It is as Paul was later to teach: 'if one part suffers, every part suffers with it; if one part is honoured, every part rejoices with it' (1 Corinthians 12:26).

## The call to the life of faith

We have now uncovered the heart of Psalm 128: the absolutely crucial importance of individual godliness. The psalm is worded in terms of a 'man' who is deeply reverent towards God, and obedient to his word. Such a man has discovered the key to personal contentment; blessedness flows from such a man out into his marriage and family, into his church, and on into the Israel of God. The truth, of course, is not confined just to the man the psalm describes; it is true for every individual in Christ. It matters whether I keep my daily tryst with the Lord; it matters whether I soak myself in his word and base my lifestyle on what he has revealed; it matters for my immediate loved ones, for the wider circle of my 'Jerusalem' and for Israel, the worldwide company of those who believe in Jesus. It matters.

Whether I like it or not – for it is the way things are by the will of God – streams flow out from me, either pure and life-giving or polluted and corrupting. The actual evidence of our eyes may not see it like that. We are not talking about a sort of 'penny in the slot' arrangement whereby we can necessarily always trace the spread of blessing, or mourn over the evidence of malign influence. The world we live in may well not be visibly like that at all – and frequently, indeed, it is not (as Job discovered)! Our position is one of faith. Psalm 1:3 says that, whatever the person devoted to Yahweh's law does, he prospers. Is it always so? Does it always seem so? If we take Psalm 1:3 as a statement of observation or of experience it is plainly false, but to do so is to misunderstand the position the psalm is adopting. We live in God's world, under the absolute rule of a totally good and benevolent Creator. It is a 'law' in his world that the good is rewarded and the bad requited. By faith we accept that as true and live accordingly. Those who come to God must believe that he exists, and that he is the rewarder of those who earnestly seek him (Hebrews 11:6).

In this way Psalm 128 calls us to the obedience of faith – to cultivate in our hearts a true fear of the Lord, and to direct our 'walk' by his revealed word. This is the way of blessing for ourselves, our relationships, our families, our church and the worldwide Israel of all believers, recalling always that, as Hebrews 6:12 says, the promises of God are a summons to 'faith and patience' until his moment of fulfilment comes.

But come it will, for (Hebrews 10:23) 'he who promised is faithful'.

---

## Notes

1 √*yare*.

2 Ezra 4:10, NIV text and margin.

3 2 Kings 17:24.

4 The NIV inexplicably represents the verb 'to fear' as 'worship' throughout this passage.

5 2 Kings 17:35–37.

6   The historical event of the exodus is used in the Old Testament to recall the Lord's work of redemption (compare Exodus 6:6), just as we use 'Calvary' or 'the cross' as a summary reference to what the Lord Jesus Christ accomplished by his death.

7   Here are a few references to illustrate what a rich vein of truth the idea of the 'fear of the Lord' offers: fear leads to obedience (Genesis 22:12); dictates a lifestyle (Job 1:1, 8); is the proper response to the word of God (Exodus 9:20); those who truly fear have no need to fear (Exodus 20:20); fear leads to praise (Psalm 22:23); to intimacy with the Lord (Psalm 25:14), to enjoyment of his goodness (31:19), care (33:18), deliverance and provision (34:7–10); etc.

8   Some discussion of the Hebrew is necessary here. NIV, NKJV, NRSV, NASB and ESV understand verses 5–6 as expressing wishes ('May the Lord bless', etc.). AV and RV offer affirmations ('The Lord shall bless . . . you shall see . . . '). On general grounds, why treat verses 5–6 as wishes when the parallel verses (2–3) are affirmations? As far as the Hebrew is concerned, verses 4–5a could be wishes, for the language does not necessarily differentiate affirmations and wishes by special forms of the verb, but in verses 5b–6a the verb 'to see' is in each case an imperative, and it is easiest to see this as an example of the imperative (the 'command' form of the verb) used to describe a consequence that will so inevitably follow that it can be commanded to happen. It is called 'the imperative of certain consequence'. Here (verses 5b–6) it is equivalent to 'And – oh yes indeed! – you will certainly see . . . ' Our exposition of the psalm, therefore, will treat the second half (verses 4–6) in the same way as the first half (verses 1–3), as affirmations.

9   The AV overplays its hand here with 'the terror of the Lord'. It is the standard noun *phobos*, 'fear' see RV, ESV.

10   'reverent' is an NIV interpretative addition.

11   Notice the (surprising) 'perhaps' in Zephaniah 2:3. It betokens a reverent and proper anxiety not to presume upon (and therefore cheapen) grace. Assurance is very far removed from cockiness.

12   Judges 6:22; 13:22; Isaiah 6:5.

13   Compare again Exodus 20:20.

14   The verb *'ashar* means 'to go straight'. This is important when we try to translate *'ashrey* in Psalm 137:8, 9. We can neither say that the man acting with brutality in war is either 'blessed' or 'happy'. Psalm 137:8–9 teaches that in God's world exact retribution is one of the governing

principles. Every good deed receives its exact reward; every evil deed its exact requital. Maybe we could therefore translate 'How right he is who . . . ' He is neither under God's blessing in committing the atrocity, nor (please God) finding personal fulfilment in what he is doing, but he is – it may well be unwittingly – implementing one of the ground rules built into Creation by its holy Creator.

15 The NIV makes verse 1 refer to 'all' but the Hebrew is in the singular, referring to each individual, as does the NKJV 'Blessed is every one . . . ' Compare verse 4, 'the man'.

16 The vine pictures richness (Genesis 49:11), joy ( Judges 9:12–13), peace (Micah 4:4; Zechariah 8:12, literally translated, calls the vine 'the seed of peace', because the vine needs settled years of peace to mature and yield), sexual attractiveness (Song of Solomon 7:8), fragrance (Song of Solomon 2:13). The vine as such is not used as a picture of fruitfulness, hence the addition here of 'fruitful'. On 'within the house', contrast Proverbs 7:11. 'Vine' and 'olive' together form a picture of joyful contentment (Deuteronomy 8:8). 'Shoots' is literally 'transplants', i.e. not chance growth but set there with deliberate intent – according to Psalm 127:3, by the Lord.

17 E.g. Hebrews 12:22–24; Revelation 21:10 – 22:5.

Psalm 129

## 13 The tonic of the backward look: How the past prepares us for the future

As far as the knocks and blows of life are concerned, its changes and chances, sorrows and sufferings, we may often be alarmed, but we should never be surprised. Alarm, yes! For the cry rises, unbidden, 'Why me? Why now? Why him or her or them? Why so awful? Why so protracted?' And so on . . . and so on . . . but we can never say we were not warned. 'We must go through many hardships', said the realistic Paul, 'to enter the kingdom of God' (Acts 14:22), thinking, of course, not in any way of paying an entrance fee, but of the road leading from conversion to glory.

It was the same for Jesus. Son though he was, 'he learned obedience from what he suffered and, once made perfect, he became the source of eternal salvation' (Hebrews 5:8–9). In his case, the purity of infant innocence made its way to the purity of mature adult holiness along the pathway of moral, spiritual choices made in the thick of the battles, challenges and hardships of this life. And in our case, as our Saviour taught, the weeds must be left beside the wheat – 'all things that offend, and those who practise lawlessness' (Matthew 13:41, NKJV) – or else the wheat will not come perfect to harvest. It is so; it has to be so. Be alarmed, if you must; do not be surprised.

## Enemies, ploughmen and furrows

When the Lord Jesus spoke of things that hurt and people who offend, he could so easily have been drawing on Psalm 129. The psalmist is looking back over the long history of Israel, starting in Israel's 'youth' in Egypt.[1] What a catalogue! Egyptian bondage, the hardships of the wilderness, the battles for the Promised Land, oppressions in the days of the Judges, Philistine wars – and then, when our ancestors came under David's and Solomon's rule and one might have hoped that peace had at last broken out, misconduct and misrule invited further disasters, invasions and oppressions.[2] It had just gone on and on without respite, and we need to remember that 'everything that was written in the past was written to teach us, so that through endurance and the encouragement of the Scriptures we might have hope' (Romans 15:4). In other words, we too are called to 'endure'; the scriptural truths from the past come to arm us with 'encouragement', so that we can face the future with 'hope'.[3]

In all this Psalm 129 is our friend and teacher.

## What a poet!

It's time we paused to take a look at the fine poem we call Psalm 129. Commentaries refer to it as an 'orphan' psalm because no author is named, but whoever wrote it must have been, like David, 'anointed by the God of Jacob', and was certainly a 'sweet psalmist of Israel'.[4] Do take time to notice how skilfully the poem has been put together. It begins with a double statement of suffering and survival (verses 1–2), and ends with a double statement (verse 8) of a life without blessing. The keynote of the first half (verses 1–3) is survival under such pitiless afflictions that they gave every appearance of succeeding in their malign purpose: 'they have not gained the victory' (verse 2);[5] the keynote of the second half (verses 6–8) is transience (verse 6), fruitlessness (verse 7) and (if there is such a word!) 'unblessedness' (verse 8). And these illustrations are not random. Ploughing should lead to growth, but not in this case: the horrid ploughing of verse 3 is balanced by the insubstantial growth of verse 6; the intensive farming of verse 3b is balanced by crop failure in verse 7; and, above all, the guardian care of a righteous God in verse 4 contrasts with life without divine blessing in verse 8.

At the centre of the psalm lies another double statement – the faithful Lord severing the cords of oppression (verse 4), and the foiled purpose and retreat of all their enemies (verse 5). The psalm opens with what is said by Israel and ends with what is not said to their would-be destroyers. What a wonderful piece of literature – but more wonderful in its truths even than in its literary qualities!

### (1) Suffering

Yes, the history of 'Israel' was one long record of recurrent suffering. It is so important always to bear in mind that it is we, who believe in Jesus, who are this Israel. We are not taking someone else's experience and making it ours at second hand or as a mere instance of what happens on earth. The 'Old Testament' is our earlier history; the psalm addresses us; and, if anything, the greater privileges that we enjoy surely invite greater adversities when we, too, constantly fall short. Also we need to remember that our Lord Jesus Christ made it plain that there is no such thing as an untested reception of the word of God. Why, even those who 'with a noble and good heart . . . hear the word' are called to 'produce a crop' by 'perseverance'.[6] It may well be the case for most of us that we have not been called to resist 'to bloodshed, striving against sin' (Hebrews 12:4, NKJV), but our ancestors were and did, and many of our brothers and sisters still are. It is part of our 'family culture'.

'Oppressed' in verses 1–2 does not strike quite the right note. It focuses attention on what the oppressor does, while the verb used[7] refers more easily to what the oppressed person feels – hostility experienced more than hostility expressed. This is the psalm's chosen starting point. The Lord's people are the object of animosity – and they feel it! Indeed, it has often been of such mammoth proportions that the only adequate illustration is a human back under the plough, scored with long furrows – a picture of humiliation (Isaiah 51:23), and destruction (Micah 3:12), but, more than anything else, of horrific cruelty (Amos 1:3).[8]

But also – reading between the lines – always purposeful.[9] This is important, for one of the things against which we are most inclined to cry out when under stress is our feeling of meaninglessness. There seems no sense in it all, and so often, to our mind, there isn't! Ask this question, then: why does Psalm 129 use agricultural illustrations? The psalm is full of them. The three in the second half of the psalm are perfectly plain. As the psalmist looked back he saw enemy after enemy as a frustrated failure – as insubstantial as wispy grass growing without root in a gutter (verse 6); too sparse even to make a handful, never mind an armful (verse 7); totally the reverse of the joyous mutuality of blessing at harvest time, as in Ruth 2:4 (verse 8). Without substance, fruit or blessedness! Well then, is the agricultural imagery of verse 3 without meaning? Certainly not. Ploughing always has a purpose. It is never an end in itself. If the soil had 'feeling', would it not cry out against such mindless brutality? But it is brutality with an end in view, for without the brutality of breaking up the fallow ground (Jeremiah 4:3) there would be no sowing, growing, maturing, reaping and harvest home!

### (2) Secret history, hidden guarantees

The people with the lacerated backs are 'Israel' (verse 1); that which excites hatred is 'Zion' (verse 5).

** 'Israel', the Lord's 'firstborn son' (Exodus 4:22), his loved and redeemed ones (Deuteronomy 7:7–8); the people among whom the Lord lives and walks (Leviticus 26:11–12), whom he shepherds (Psalm 80:1), and guards with tender care as the apple of his eye (Deuteronomy 32:10; Zechariah 2:8), doubly and trebly more honoured and prized now in its final realization as those redeemed by the precious blood of God's own Son (Galatians 3:13–14, 26–29).
** 'Zion', God's 'holy hill' (Psalm 2:6), his dwelling place (Psalm 9:11), his guarded (Psalm 48:12–14), loved (Psalm 87:2), and chosen (Psalm 132:13) city; furthermore, the location of his 'house' to which his people 'draw near' through the blood of the sacrifices he has ordained[10] – doubly and trebly more honoured and prized now in its final realization as the heavenly Jerusalem, the present city of those who belong to Jesus, the mediator of a new covenant, and live under his sprinkled blood (Hebrews 12:22–24), the locus of their citizenship (Philippians 3:20–21), and the eternal city of those whose names are in the Lamb's book of life (Revelation 21:22–27).

Little did Israel's and Zion's enemies know what they were meddling with. Even the beleaguered Hezekiah realized that Sennacherib was 'ridiculing the living God' (Isaiah 37:4), and how right Isaiah was, on that same occasion, while the Assyrians were still swollen with triumphalism, to see 'the virgin daughter of Zion' tossing her head in derision, because their hostile eyes had been raised in pride 'against the Holy One of Israel' (Isaiah 37:22, 23)! The world's opposition is some-times openly expressed but always simmering away against Jesus' people (John 15:18–21), and their focused hatred is always reserved for the precious blood by which we have been saved, and which is our standing ground before God for all eternity. Nevertheless, Israel is always his protected species, and Zion is already the heavenly city, far above mere human interference.

### (3) The righteous Lord (verse 4)

The security of Israel and Zion is neither accidental nor negotiable. It is 'all down to' 'the LORD' who 'is righteous'. As we pointed out above, the centre ground of the psalm is occupied by divine action cancelling out what enemies have done (verse 4) and sending them packing, with their intentions frustrated (verse 5).[11] The Hebrew says only that the Lord has 'cut the cords of the wicked' (compare NKJV). The NIV may be correct in interpreting this as freeing from bonds one who has been captured and fettered. In the context of the ploughing metaphor of verse 3, however, the severed cords could be the harness on the plough animals, thereby destroying the capacity of the enemy to inflict further hurt.[12] Either way, the Lord is the agent. His divine Name, Yahweh,[13] first explained to Moses, declares him to be eternally (Exodus 3:15) the God who redeems his people and destroys his enemies,[14] and his character as 'righteous' proclaims that this is the invariable rule and motivation controlling all he does.

### (4) The past and the future

'Past' and 'future' sum up the balance of Psalm 129. The opening verses look back. Against all human odds, and time after time, enemies ground

Israel under foot, but it was Israel that saw the last of them, not the other way round. The seemingly unconquerable tide of Assyrian imperialism rolled in against Jerusalem, lapping up to the very walls, and receded more quickly than it had arisen, never to threaten again.[15]

Against such a history of human danger and divine deliverance, how does one face the future (129:5–8)? Verses 5–8 are intended to answer this question, but do they do so as a prayer or as an affirmation? The Hebrew does not offer us an answer, only a choice. The verses may be a prayer, they may affirm – or, best of all, we may take them both ways, each expressing a valuable truth.

If they are a prayer, then this is how to face a future that is likely to prove every bit as menacing as the past ever was. Face it in prayer, as John Newton taught:

> His love in times past forbids me to think
> He'll leave me at last in trouble to sink . . .
> By prayer let me wrestle and he will perform,
> With Christ in the vessel I'll smile at the storm.[16]

Don't be afraid of such vigorous, realistic prayers! This is the way to commit life-threatening situations to God, for it is praying in accordance with what he has taught in his word is the right thing to happen: people who would bring unjustified trouble on someone else deserve that they should themselves suffer what they wished to inflict (Deuteronomy 19:15–21). The enemy, who treated Israel as a mere thing, a field to be ploughed for their own profit, intended to leave Zion as feeble as rooftop grass, as meagre as a failed harvest, and as if it were not the place of the Lord's blessing. To baulk at praying for a similar fate to befall an oppressor is to reveal either that one has never been in danger of one's life, or that one lacks the imagination to feel what it would be like.

If prayer is the way to face the future, faith is the way to walk into it. The Lord who has acted so wonderfully in the past has laid down his own parameters of action. He does not change. Look the approaching danger in the face; no weapon forged against us will prevail (Isaiah 54:17); God is still on the throne. The sceptre of wickedness will not remain over the land allotted to the righteous (Psalm 125:3). 'The Church is an anvil that has worn out many hammers'[17] – or, if you prefer it, 'the Lord is righteous' (verses 4–5), always on the side of his people, cutting the cords of oppression, frustrating hostile intentions.

---

## Notes

1   E.g. Jeremiah 2:1–3; Hosea 11:1 (NIV 'child' would be better as 'young man', 'lad', or 'youth', a word directly related to the word in Psalm 129:1–2).

2   E.g. Exodus 1:14; 16:3; Joshua 12; Judges 6:2–5; 1 Samuel 4; 2 Samuel 5:17–25; 11:27; 14 – 18; 1 Kings 11; 12:16–19; 2 Kings 17; 24 – 25; etc.

3   Colloquially we use the word 'hope' ('I hope it will be fine tomorrow') to express certainty as to time ('tomorrow') but uncertainty as to experience ('it will be fine'). In the Bible, 'hope' expresses certainty as to experience, uncertainty as to time – e.g. 'the hope of the glory of God' will certainly be our experience, but 'when' is known only to him.

4   Compare 2 Samuel 23.1. Alec Motyer, *Treasures of the King* (IVP, 2007), pp. 151ff.

5   Literally (not 'but') '– also' (NKJV 'Yet'), as if to say, when all their ferocity has been taken into account, there is 'also' this surprising fact – 'they have not been able for me'. Somehow or other there is a superior power resident in the Lord's people. Not a certificate of immunity, but a guarantee of superiority. Compare Isaiah 10:27 (NKJV); 1 John 4:4. See Motyer, *Isaiah*, TOTC (IVP, 1999), p. 101.

6   Luke 8:15. The parable of the sower (as we call it) is pre-eminently the parable of the tested seed. What the NIV translates as 'perseverance' is *hypomonē*, endurance. Compare 1 Thessalonians 2:13–14, where Paul teaches that consequent suffering is a mark of the genuineness of our acceptance of the word of God.

7   √*tsarar*: compare Numbers 33:55, (give you trouble); Judges 11:7 (in trouble); 1 Samuel 13:6 ('their situation was critical', NKJV 'in danger').

8   2 Samuel 12:31 contains the sad possibility that such methods were used against captives of war (see RV). But see discussion in Baldwin, *1 and 2 Samuel*, TOTC (IVP, 1988), p. 246.

9   David Dickson, *The Psalms* (Banner of Truth, 1959), p. 433, sounds a trifle 'quaint' to our ears, but his comment is to the point: 'What the enemies do against the church, the Lord maketh use of for maturing the church, which is his field; albeit they intend no good to God's church, yet they

serve God's wisdom to prepare the Lord's people for receiving the seed of God's word.

10  Compare Exodus 29:42–46; Leviticus 1:1; Psalm 43:3–4.

11  In the OT shame (√*bos*), while it always retained the idea of embarrassment, usually has the predominant meaning of 'disappointment', failure of what was hoped for, promised or intended.

12  Compare the broken snare of 124:7.

13  Notice the four upper-case letters, LORD, which always represent the 'Name', i.e. a shorthand declaration of all the God of Israel has revealed about himself in his own person as the God of salvation – the incognito Old Testament revelation of God the Holy Trinity, Father, Son and Holy Spirit.

14  Exodus 6:2, 6, 8; 14:18, 30–31.

15  2 Kings 18:13 – 19:37; 2 Chronicles 32 – 33; Isaiah 36 – 37; Psalm 48 could well be a meditation on this experience – that Zion should remain unscathed after such a threat (verse 12)!

16  From John Newton's hymn, 'Begone, unbelief! My Saviour is near'.

17  See Wilcock, Vol 2., p. 237.

Psalm 130

# 14 Out of the depths into the light: The inside story

Martin Luther counted Psalm 130 among his favourites, giving it the (to him) supreme accolade of 'Pauline'. In other words, he found the psalm full of characteristic emphases beloved of the apostle Paul:

** humans, by nature, are under condemnation because of their sin (Ephesians 2:1–3);
** mercy is free (Romans 3:23, 24; Ephesians 2:4–5);
** redemption is a spiritual matter, redemption from sin (Romans 6:5–6; Colossians 1:21);[1]
** and, we ought to add in fairness to Paul as well as to the psalm, salvation is all of God (2 Corinthians 5:18–21; Titus 3:4–6).

With many thanks to Martin Luther for this 'pointer', these four truths are, in fact, an excellent way into the teaching of Psalm 130.

## Condemnation: The human tragedy

Psalms 129 – 131 make up the fourth 'triad' in the Songs of the Great Ascent, which continues in the spirit of its immediate predecessor,

Psalms 126 – 128. The first two triads were songs of pilgrims to Zion – starting in an uncongenial, hostile world (120, 123), finding the Lord sufficient for the perils of the pilgrim way (121, 124) and coming into the blessedness and safety of the city that was their goal (122, 125). The third triad announced a new perspective by starting in Zion (126:1), but, more particularly, a Zion not yet what it would some day be (126:4), a place of blessing, but with its true, full harvest, with all its joys, yet to come (126:6). We expressed this as a 'pilgrimage of the heart' – already in Zion but still longing for Zion. In that third triad, the pilgrims' problem was the enmity of a hostile, uncongenial world, an experience continuing in its most brutal forms in Psalm 129. But there is another side to the same story: the fundamental necessity to be right with God, to be confident of it, and, because of this, to be fully assured of the final outcome – for what is the point of external calm if the problem of the heart is not solved? What is the point of seeing the end of earthly opposition if we are not at peace with God? And, if we can be as certain as the pilgrim psalms are that every problem of hostility and opposition will succumb to divine power and authority, can we be equally sure that the Lord will deal with the problem of sin?

For it is a problem. It is like being caught and held in a watery waste of glutinous mire. This is the very first word of the psalm – 'out of the depths'. Psalm 69 speaks of 'waters up to the neck' (verse 1), of sinking into a miry depth of mud with no foothold (verse 2), and (verse 3) of being in the 'deep waters' (our word in 130:1) of the sea, at the mercy of its rip tides and undertows. So that's where our psalmist is, and the problem is not life's troubles, whether general or particular, but his own 'iniquities' (verse 3, NIV, 'sins', likewise in verse 8). This is what leaves the psalmist without a foothold (verse 3, 'stand'; compare 69:2),[2] and, now, not in a metaphorical sea of trouble, but, because of sin, without a secure standing in the presence of God. The problem is more than individual; it reappears when he addresses his whole people (verse 8). No one has 'standing'[3] before God as long as 'iniquity' remains an unresolved matter. To be and continue before him, to attend upon him, and to offer him service – all these are out of the question while 'iniquity' remains.

In the vocabulary of sin in the Old Testament, 'iniquity' is what we *are* rather than what we *do*. It pursues the question of sin into our constitution. Pictorially, we are like warped timber.[4] 'Iniquity' is the 'bent' of our nature towards sin, wrongdoing and rebellion against the law of God. In a word, it is 'the fallen nature', which we can no more change, of ourselves, than we can cease to be human. What we are by nature traps us in hopelessness and condemnation.

## Mercy: The Lord's two companions

Have you ever sung:

> 'Oh, the love that drew salvation's plan!
> Oh, the grace that brought it down to man!
> Oh, the mighty gulf that God did span at Calvary!
> Mercy there was great and grace was free;
> Pardon there was multiplied to me;
> There my burdened soul found liberty,
> At Calvary.'?[5]

Probably not! But don't you wish you had? Aren't the words worth singing? The 'liberty' they speak of is not, of course, the political freedom spoken of so much today, but freedom from our natural entrapment in sin and condemnation. The divine 'pardon' and 'love' that bring that liberty are exactly what the psalmist extolled in Psalm 130.

** 'But with you there is forgiveness' (verse 4). The wonderful – and, indeed, mysterious – thing is that it is the nature of God that binds us in condemnation, and the same nature of God that brings us release. If the Lord our God were not holy, sin would not matter; if the Lord our God took no notice of sin, our long record of wrongdoing, rebellion and unworthiness would not matter. But he is holy,[6] and he does know all there is to know about us;[7] he hates sin, and is angered ceaselessly by it.[8] This is the problem: not sin as a nuisance and blight within human life and relationships, but sin as the object of divine detestation, anger, and hostility.

Psalm 130 speaks for the whole Bible when it says (literally), 'but with you is the forgiveness'. It is the Lord's constant companion; and it is the genuine article – 'the' forgiveness, that is, such a forgiveness as can deal with whatever the need is, a forgiveness that satisfies the divine nature and meets the human need, the only forgiveness truly worthy of the name.[9]

** 'For with the Lord is unfailing love' (verse 7). The Lord certainly keeps excellent company! Alongside his first companion, 'forgiveness', there is a second, 'unfailing love'. The Hebrew word is *chesedh*, one of the truly 'big' words of the Bible.[10] A couple fall in love and plan to get married. This love is a heartfelt emotion from each towards the other. At their wedding, however, they pledge a love 'for better, for worse, for richer, for poorer, in sickness and in health, till death do us part', and they publicly affirm this sort of love for each other by saying, in turn, 'I will'. It is love centred in the will; it is a settled commitment, not fluctuating with the emotions, but unchanging. This is *chesedh*, the Lord's unchangeable commitment to his people, his 'ever-unchanging' love. Like 'the forgiveness' in verse 4, verse 7 records literally 'the unfailing love', and the use of the definite article has the same significance. Here is love that is love indeed. In human experience the totally sincere lifelong commitment made on the wedding day can prove to be as transient as the emotional quickening that first drew a couple to each other. In our case, the will is as much infected with the virus of sin as is the heart, and (as Hosea 6:4 says) our *chesedh* – our 'ever-unfailing love' – is 'like the morning mist, like early dew that disappears'. Not his! His ever-unfailing love is the genuine article, love as only divine love can be.

### Redemption: A third companion

** Literally, 'and to an abundant degree, with him is redemption' (verse 7), with the consequence that 'He will, himself, redeem Israel from all his iniquities' (verse 8, NIV, 'sins'). Both the noun (*p⁽ᶜ⁾duth*) and its verb (√*padah*) have a broad meaning of protective care in adversity, but in the psalm they specify a very particular care: the Lord's 'abundant' capacity to protect and rescue; more accurately, to ransom his people from iniquity and its consequences.[11] This ransoming work is spiritual, a spiritual salvation. In other words, the Lord has found a 'ransom price' which, on the one hand, satisfies his holiness and appeases his wrath and, on the other hand, releases his unfailing love to flow out, unchecked, to the guilty soul.

## All of God: Non-contributory salvation

Faced with this huge problem of salvation, and the sheer impossibility of a sinner 'standing' before the Lord (verse 3), the psalmist's *reaction* is to pray (verses 1–2), and his *attitude* is to wait (verses 5–6). There is no proposal for personal reformation; no adoption of a new 'rule of life' whereby past misdeeds might be balanced – and, one would hope, cancelled out – by present and future good deeds. If salvation is to come, it must come from God (therefore pray). Additionally, it is wholly dependent on divine decision and action (therefore wait).

** As regards prayer: first, even the deepest depths of sin constitute no barrier to praying (verse 1); sinner though I am, I can call to the Lord in my own person, and with my own voice (verse 2a). This is because I am seeking 'mercy' (verse 2b) – rather, better, 'grace'.[12] Sin and need are the occasion of prayer; the sinner is the voice of prayer, and grace is the basis on which prayer rests.

** As regards waiting, two verbs are used in the psalm (verses 5–7), but they are synonymous, with the shared meaning 'to wait with confident expectation'.[13] Such 'waiting', such sustained expectancy, is not easy. Verse 5, so to speak, 'tails off' into verse 6, as though waiting had become a weariness, a holding-on to hope even when hope seems as slow to come as morning when night is at its darkest. We can render the psalm more literally like this:

> verse 5, I wait confidently for the Lord;
> My soul waits confidently;
> And for/on his word I continue in expectancy –
> verse 6, My soul for the Sovereign One,
> More than watchmen for the morning,
> watchmen for the morning!

See how verbs disappear in verse 6, as though there was only enough energy to express the bare facts! Nevertheless, confidence, even if holding on by its fingernails, is sure. First, it looks to the Lord's word. If we translate 'on his word', then certainty of hope is nourished by some truth the Lord has already revealed or some promise he has already made. If we translate 'for his word', then hope is confidently directed to the Lord himself, waiting for him to speak the word of release and salvation. This, in Psalm 130, is a particularly sure ground. The last word of verse 1 is 'LORD' (Yahweh); the first word in verse 2 is 'Lord' (Sovereign One).[14] See how the same pairing occurs in verse 3, and in verses 5–6. 'Yahweh' is the God who revealed the meaning of his personal name in the Exodus (3:15; 6:6) – the God who redeems his people. To link Yahweh with Adonai, Sovereign, is to say that only he can decide to save, and that, once he sets himself to save, nothing can stand in his way; he is sovereign in salvation. Furthermore, in verse 3 'LORD' stands for a form of Yahweh, 'Yah', shortened as a sign of intimacy and endearment, a plain hint that (as Paul is yet to put it in Romans 5:20) 'where sin increased, grace increased all the more'. And, finally, in verses 7–8 where 'confident waiting' is the desired mark of the people of God, only 'the LORD' is mentioned – twice by name, twice by pronoun. That is all that is needed: the simple memory of, and steady eye fixed on, the God of our salvation, the LORD of all grace. It is a correct emphasis when verse 8 says 'He himself'. Only he can save. Himself, he undertakes the whole task of our salvation.

---

## Notes

1  To this point the material about Luther is based on F. Delitzsch, *Biblical Commentary on The Psalms*, Vol. III (T. & T. Clark, 1881), p. 302.

2  NIV 'foothold' is a noun from the verb 'to stand' used in 130:3.

3  'Standing' was the way Elijah expressed his sense of acceptance, and, so to speak, permanence in the presence of the Lord (1 Kings 17:1; 18:15, etc. Not, as NIV, 'whom I serve', but, NKJV, 'before whom I stand'). Compare Jeremiah 15:1; 23:18, 22. Against the possibility of such 'standing' there is the Lord's holiness (1 Samuel 6:20), glory (1 Kings 8:11, literally, 'to stand to minister') and anger (Psalm 76:7).

4  The noun translated 'iniquity' (*'awon*) is derived from the verb $\sqrt{}$*awah*, to bend, twist. For the basic vocabulary of sin, see Alec Motyer, *Treasures of the King: Psalms from the Life of David* (IVP, 2007), p. 120.

5 No. 135, *C.S.S.M. Choruses* No. 1 (Novello, 1936). Words by
W. R. Newell.

6 Psalm 22:3; Isaiah 43:15. The adjective 'holy' is used with the Lord's
Name, more often than all other adjectives put together (e.g. Psalm
103:1). In the Bible 'holy' is pretty well equivalent to the divine nature;
it is the quality that infuses all else that is true of the Lord.

7 E.g. Joshua 22:22, 23; Psalms 44:21; 94:11; 138:6.

8 Psalms 5:5–6; 45:7; Psalm 7:11.

9 Noun *s<sup>e</sup>liychah*. The verb, √*salach*, occurs forty-six times, always of an
act of God, never of human forgiveness. Forgiveness comes in answer
to request (1 Kings 8:20); for the sake of the Lord's Name (Psalm 25:11);
following repentance (Isaiah 55:7, NIV 'freely' is, in fact, 'abundantly');
based on sacrifice / atonement (Leviticus 4:22–23; Numbers 15:25, 28);
an attribute of the Lord (Psalm 103:3).

10 Alec Motyer, *Treasures*, as above, pp. 120–121. In Genesis 19:19 (its first
occurrence), 'kindness' is the product of 'favour' (grace). It is the Lord
standing by his covenant with Abraham, see verse 29; Exodus 34:6 links
'love' (*chesedh*) and 'faithfulness', reliability, truth to himself; Exodus
15:13, the Lord's faithful care of his redeemed; Deuteronomy 7:9,
covenant-keeping; Psalm 118:1–3, enduring love.

11 For the noun, see Exodus 8:23<19>. In Psalm 111:9 'redemption' is a
covenant act of the Lord. Compare Dickson, 'So many straits as the
Lord's people can fall into, so many escapes and deliverances hath the
Lord in store for them.' In Isaiah 50:2 the NIV offers the translation
'ransom'. This is derived from the 'parent' verb √*padah*, which is used
of care in a wide variety of troubles (e.g. 2 Samuel 4:9, 'delivered') but,
more particularly, it means 'ransom' – by payment (e.g. Leviticus 27:27;
Exodus 13:13 with Numbers 3:45–48 and 18:15–16).

12 A plural noun, *tach<sup>a</sup>nunim*, possibly a plural of plenitude or
abundance. The parent verb is *chanan*, to be gracious, giving rise to
the simple noun *chen*, 'grace' (its first occurrence is in Genesis 6:8),
exactly as in the New Testament, the sheer unmerited, undeserved
favour of God.

13 In verse 5 'wait' translates √*qawah* and in verses 5, 7 'hope' translates
√*yachal*: in form the first occurrence (NIV 'put my hope', verse 5, *hiphil*)
suggests 'adopt a waiting posture / attitude', 'practise waiting', and the
second (verse 7, *piel*) be 'busy waiting' – a striking oxymoron, i.e., 'be
committed to waiting', or 'simply wait'. As far as the verbs are

concerned the translations 'wait' and 'hope' could be switched. Both verbs express confidence in expectancy.

14 I.e. *Adonai*, always represented by a single upper-case letter 'Lord', a title, 'Sovereign One', just as Yahweh (the personal Name) is always four upper-case letters, 'LORD'.

Psalm 131

# 15 At peace: Never stop being a child

It's one thing for an adult to be childish – and, unfortunately, all too possible! It's quite another thing to be child*like* – and that takes a lot of working at! There you are, then. In one sentence we have given away the whole secret of Psalm 131.

**Babies are beautiful – most of the time!**

There is no easier moment for tears than when you hold your baby for the first time – maybe just moments after birth. So tiny, so wonderful, so beautiful! Yes, all that. Tears of wonder, of thankfulness, of joy. But so often very different feelings prevail when howls in the night disrupt the sleep you think you so dreadfully need! Those howls can sound shockingly bad-tempered, but actually they are not. Howls are the only means your tiny treasure has at that moment of sharing distress – usually hunger, though, in far-off days, sometimes a clumsily placed nappy pin! Not bad temper, then, just forcibly expressed demand, a self-concern that may yet become self-centredness.

What the infant knows is not the market law of supply and demand, but the family law of demand and supply. It is the art of parenthood to guide and shape babyhood into toddlerhood, and, when it happens, it is lovely to see. Mum is no longer there to meet demand; it is enough that she is there; not now the breast to feed, but the hand to hold, the cuddle that assures, the kiss that makes it better.

That is the picture with which the heart of the psalm illustrates its message (verse 2). The child has been weaned; the days of breast and bottle are over. In the family, the little one now occupies a high chair at the family table, and tucks into appropriate 'solids'; but time and again the toys that are so treasured are left, and off the small figure trots to make sure mother is still around. That's all that is needed. The inarticulate howl for food has become the question 'Will you read me a story?' – which is, so often, only a way of expressing the deeper, instinctive, need: can I come and sit on your knee, and feel your arms around me, and hear your voice?[1]

**The childlike soul**

The word most often translated 'soul' (*nephesh*) is as versatile in shades of meaning as any word in the whole Bible – too much so for us to follow up here. But it is frequently an all-purpose word for the mixture of emotions, passions, desires, appetites (and faculties) that makes up our inner person. As far as Psalm 131 is concerned, Allen puts his finger on the spot when he paraphrases the *nephesh* as the 'headstrong self'.[2] And we all know all too much about that! The hymn-writer could recall 'fightings and fears within, without';[3] James (4:1) put it forcefully when he wrote of 'your desires that battle within you' – or, even more strongly, 'your pleasures/delights that are on active military service in your members'. Every believer is a battleground, with the battle surging this way and that – the 'mind' serving the law of God, the flesh the law of sin (Romans 7:25), the 'sinful nature' and 'the Spirit' constantly at odds (Galatians 5:17), each entertaining desires in irreconcilable opposition to the other, or, recalling the first way this was expressed, when the Lord God addressed the usurping serpent, 'I will put enmity between you and the woman, and between your offspring and hers' (Genesis 3:15). This is the situation that sin and the fall created: the dislocation of human personality consequent on that first, damaging, disobedience. It has, of course, been solved and settled by Jesus when, on the cross

(Hebrews 10:12–14), he both bore our sin and conquered our Adversary (and when the Lord Jesus returns we will enter at last into the full experience of that once-for-all sin-bearing and conquest), but, in the meantime, becoming Christians introduces us into the field of battle at a more furious, constant and challenged level than was ever the case while were merely 'in the flesh'. To be sure, every spiritual blessing has already been given, sufficient for time and eternity, but the blessing is ours only 'in the heavenly realms' (Ephesians 1:3), precisely the sphere in which we battle not with flesh and blood but with 'rulers . . . authorities . . . powers of this dark world . . . spiritual forces of evil in the heavenly realms' (Ephesians 6:12).

## Spiritual responsibility

One particular battlefield in this truly cosmic conflict of ours is identified in Psalm 131: the battle for our own soul. In David's experience,[4] the soul is as turbulent as a stormy sea that needs 'quelling' (verse 2, NIV 'stilled'),[5] as 'rough going' as an uneven, rutted road that needs resurfacing. The even tenor of personal life is disrupted, thrown into turmoil by restless, attention-seeking feelings and impulses, thoughts and objectives. And there was more: his soul was loud in demanding the immediate satisfaction of his needs and claims (NIV 'quietened').[6] It had all the crying, instinctive, characteristics of an infant.

## Decision time

What, then, is to be done about this? Are we to remain infants or progress towards maturity? Will we allow ourselves to be stuck for ever in the pram and never take to our own legs and walk? The answer is too obvious to put into words, but the key question is 'How?' See what the psalm says: 'I have stilled . . . (I have) quietened.' The task and the responsibility fall squarely on each one of us. It is not like 'salvation', where we stand still and the Lord undertakes all (Exodus 14:13; Titus 3:5); it is 'sanctification', in which those whom the Lord has made alive from the dead (Romans 6:13) are called to get up and function, to leave the pram and start walking,[7] to live out the new life they have been given in Christ.

If my 'soul' is to be 'quelled' and 'silenced', it is up to me to see to it.


## Replication (not repetition)

With all this in mind, it is striking that 131:3 repeats the 'call' of 130:7 to 'put our hope in the Lord'/'adopt an attitude of expectant, patient, sustained "waiting" on and for him'. In Psalm 130, that was how our salvation came about: the only way to deal with our desperate problem of sin was to turn and wait for the solution from the God whom our sin offended, enraged and alienated. Now Psalm 131 tells us to adopt the same attitude in relation to a very different problem: how I am to make headway with God against the turbulence of my own soul. Oh yes, the responsibility now rests on me; and, yes indeed, I am called to make the decisive moves in the battle to quell the turbulence and silence the demands, but I will make any headway in this task only if I am constantly replicating the relationship with the Lord that, at the beginning, brought me salvation.

Careful thought is required here. Once we have been truly saved we can never be 'unsaved'. Even in human terms, though a parent may want to disown a child (and vice versa) the relationship itself of parent–child and child–parent can never be unpicked. So it is when, through Christ, we become the children of God (John 1:12). The relationship itself carries eternal consequences (1 John 3:1–2). The two-handed grip of Father and Son will never be relaxed, nor its claim to possession abandoned to another (John 10:28, 29). No, we are not to 'repeat' our salvation. That issue has been settled, but 'waiting on the Lord', 'waiting on and for his word' (130:5) is intended to be our permanent stance before him and our unchanging relationship to him (Isaiah 40:31). This is the life setting in which the toddler grows; this is what gives toddlers confidence for living, a sure and secure context for life, and a platform for advancing to the next stage: keeping company with the great Parent, feeling the strength of his hand gripping ours (Psalm 73:23, 24), knowing that he will never leave or forsake us, or lead us astray. Cultivating the presence, enjoying the companionship, resting on the promises, listening out for the word – and one more thing (where Psalm 131 starts) speaking to him, telling him all about it, what we have attempted, what we hope to achieve, and where we will continue to stand.

A friend once confessed that he was not of that 'stamp' that found it possible to spend two or three hours at a stretch in serious prayer, but, he said, 'Most times of the day you will find me nattering to the Lord'. Well, of course, he may very possibly have been wrong to abandon the struggle for extended times of prayer. Did he not know about the battle for the soul? Was he just acquiescing in the face of conflict? All that is for him to say. But was he not setting us an example when he filled every odd moment of the day with 'nattering to the Lord'? Companionship is more than 'set piece' occasions. It is the relaxed, conscious enjoyment of another's company. It is the bliss of a small child holding its mother's hand. So David walked at peace with the Lord – 'a weaned child with its mother'; so David walked at peace with himself – 'like a weaned child my soul is within me'. The restlessness was stilled, the disruptive elements quieted, the demanding cries hushed.

**Know the Lord; know your enemy**

The psalm singles out three areas in which the victory has to be won: (verse 1), the heart, the eyes, and the busy round of life.

(1) *The heart*. In our common usage, 'heart' – as in the phrase 'affairs of the heart' – stands for our emotions. In the Old Testament its coverage is pretty well as wide as that of the 'soul'. 'The heart' is every facet of the hidden life of the personality, what a person is, does, feels and thinks 'on the inside'.

** Proverbs 4:23 offers a deep insight into biblical psychology: 'Above all else, guard your heart, for it is the wellspring of life.' Everything starts there; life springs out of what we are at the hidden centre.
** Jesus reinforced the same truth, with even greater emphasis on the heart as the potent life-changer: Matthew 23:26, 'First clean the inside of the cup . . . then the outside also will be clean.'
** The heart that 'gets above itself'[8] (this, I would suggest, is what the verb 'to be high' means here) is the primary battleground. It is so

terribly easy to put on a show of having a properly lowly self-estimate, but, at the very same moment, to be inwardly sure how much better we are than the person we are talking to! Self-denigration can become a habit that is no more than top dressing over a sorely proud spirit.[9]
** One more thing: the clue to a change of heart. When the Emmaus walkers talked together in their home after Jesus had left them and before they set out to go back to Jerusalem, they said: 'Were not our hearts burning within us while he talked with us on the road and opened the Scriptures to us?' (Luke 24:32). What an insight for us into the way things work! The 'slow heart' (Luke 24:25) became the burning heart through hearing and understanding the word of God in the context of the companionship of Jesus.

(2) *The eyes.* The Old Testament has a way of using physical things to express moral truths – like the verb 'to be high' expressing pride. So the 'eyes' can, for example, express the other side of self-importance[10] – as in our expression 'to look down on'. If that is the meaning here, then we are first warned to guard our hearts against an unwarrantedly high view of ourselves, and now to avoid an unwarrantedly low view of everyone else – like the Pharisee in our Lord's parable, who was confident of his own righteousness and 'looked down on everyone else' (Luke 18:8).

But the eye is also the organ of desire.[11] In Psalm 123:2 we met the longing eye of the servant fixed on the master. In Psalm 101:3 David pledges that he will 'set before [his] eyes no vile thing'. In this sense, then, the words (literally) 'my eyes are not exalted' could be a disavowal of overambition, 'setting one's sights high' – on one side, a constant spirit of discontent with the way things are; on the other side, an obsessive determination to achieve the 'glittering prizes'; very far from that spirit of restful contentment that Paul was so delighted to have learned (Philippians 4:12), the positive New Testament counterpart of the Tenth Commandment (Exodus 20:17).

(3) *Occupations and preoccupations.* In verse 1, 'concern' is possibly a little less energetic, and more bland, than the word requires. Maybe, 'busy myself with', 'be preoccupied with'[12] – or, to paraphrase, 'I do not allow my life to be taken over by schemes I know I could never achieve or problems I know I can never solve.' I confess that I am easier in mind

about the latter part of that paraphrase than the former. 'Wonderful' can, as a word, just mean 'beyond human capacity' (Deuteronomy 17:8), but the whole group of words to which it belongs is vastly more often used of the Lord.[13] Probably, therefore 'great matters' may be taken to refer to earthly, human projects, while 'wonderful' will more naturally refer to questions within the divine sphere, for the word is the nearest thing to 'supernatural' that Hebrew contains. We talk about someone 'running after hares', wasting time on targets that everyone can see will never be hit, projects that will inevitably come to nothing, big ideas far and away out of all proportion, while more mundane avenues of effectiveness are ignored and neglected. It is a form of unrealism in self-appraisal. And there are also people who are all too ready to get hung up on insoluble theological questions: stop the world, I've got a problem – in fact they often seem to think that 'having problems' is the sign of being a 'real person'. Moses wisely said, 'The secret things belong to the Lord our God, but the things revealed belong to us' (Deuteronomy 29:29). There is a point – indeed, it comes over and over again – at which our task is to learn to live with unsolved conundrums, resting upon the huge volume of truth that has been revealed to us in Scripture, and upon the Lord God who has revealed himself as totally trustworthy, and with whom whatever 'bugs' us may be safely left.

### 'That I may know him' (Philippians 3:10, NKJV)

Psalm 131 opens with the divine Name, Yahweh, as its first word (verse 1) and ends with the words, literally, 'Yahweh, now and for eternity' (verse 3). When we notice this lovely 'bracket' round the psalm, we see the immense truth surrounding the simple picture of the weaned child with its mother. My soul, too, has a parent, with all the qualities of the finest maternal/paternal love and care, and his name is Yahweh, the God who revealed himself when he came down to redeem his people, and who has never ceased to be our great and divine Next-of-Kin. For all eternity this will be our portion, living in his presence, resting in his care, and our present task is to say, 'As then, so now'. To make today a heaven on earth by savouring, cultivating and resting contentedly in his company, as his child who never grew up.

## Notes

1 In verse 2, 'with its mother' (compare RV, NKJV) is correct, as against, e.g. NASB, 'rests against/upon its mother'. The preposition *al* most often means 'on, upon', but is regularly used to mean 'beside' (Genesis 16:7, NIV 'near'; 18:2 NIV, 'nearby', literally, 'beside him'). Verse 2 should read 'like a weaned child is my soul beside me'; compare NRSV, as against NIV, NKJV, 'within'.

2 L. C. Allen, *Psalms 101–150* (Word, 1987), p. 199.

3 Charlotte Elliott, 'Just as I am, without one plea'.

4 There is no need to question David's authorship of this psalm. Even in his later days, when his kingliness often rather went to his head, and when he became a somewhat remote father figure to his polygamous household (note how his own daughter refers to him as 'the king', 2 Samuel 13:13!), he must have enjoyed many of his better moments of high spiritual ambition and longing, but his earlier days, and the whole period when he accepted Saul's kingship, often under extreme provocation, provide ample opportunity for a psalm such as this.

5 √*shawah*, to be equal to, or 'equable', to smooth something out, to compose something turbulent. E.g. Isaiah 28:25, to level a field for sowing.

6 √*damam*, to be motionless, at rest, quiet, silent – both senses of 'still'. In usage, 'silence' predominates (fifteen out of twenty-four occurrences). In verse 2, 'stilled' and 'quieted' are in the Hebrew 'perfect' tense. We could, therefore, interpret them as 'perfects of determination': 'I have determined to . . .', a resolute joining of battle.

7 'Walk' is a striking New Testament verb of getting on with living our new life in Christ. See AV (and, for all the references except the first, NKJV) Ephesians 4:1, 17; 5:2, 8, 15); NIV, 'live'.

8 'not proud' (v.1), lit., 'is not high', √*gabah*, e.g. 2 Chronicles 26:16; Proverbs 18:12; Ezekiel 28:2, 5, 17.

9 Romans 12:16 is only one of many New Testament verses commanding a properly lowly self-estimate. In Ephesians 4:2; Philippians 2:3; Colossians 3:12, NIV 'humble, humility' is, more literally, 'humble-minded', a word of inner self-appraisal and realism, a constant NT target for the believer.

10 E.g. Psalms 18:27; 101:5.

11 Job 31:1, 16; Ezekiel 24:16, 21.

12 The intensive (*piel*) form of the verb √*halach*, to go, walk. The 'fundamental idea' of the *piel* mode is 'to busy oneself eagerly with' (*Gesenius Hebrew Grammar* [Oxford, 1910], p. 141).

13 The verb √*pala'*, to be extraordinary, wonderful; noun, *pele'*, a 'wonder'; adj., *pilᵉ'i*, 'wonderful'.

## Psalms 132 – 134
## 16 Take a break: Look back, look on

Of course, seeing 'the Songs of the Ascent' as a hymn book for pilgrims going up to the temple festivals is far from being the only way of looking at them. There are not quite as many interpretations as there are commentators, but, none the less, there are plenty.[1] However, to understand the psalms as a hymn book for pilgrims has a nice simplicity about it, and, as I have tried to show, it 'works'.

The first two 'triads' (groups of three, 120 – 122, 123 – 125) kept the pilgrims' *pathway* before us. We are on our way out of this uncongenial world (120, 123), finding the Lord sufficient for the rigours and hazards of the journey (121, 124), and heading for the bliss of Zion (122, 125), with all its perfection and security.

But there is another side to being a pilgrim, for not all the difficulties of our journey are external. There are inner demons to be fought, inner inadequacies to be put right, and inner problems demanding solution. It was to this side of things that the next two triads (126 – 128, 129 – 131) turned. Oh yes, we have experienced salvation, but we are still waiting to be saved (126); the trials we endure can also involve intense personal pain and distress (129); there are personal, domestic and social problems (127), and, above all, there is the chronic problem of sin (130). Yet, there is still blessing from Zion to cover all our days (128) and the calm bliss of peace with God (131).

Now there is one triad left (132 – 134), the last group of the Songs of the Great Ascent. These are the songs of those who have arrived and are safe at home. All three psalms are dominated by the reality of Zion: first, it is the city of the Lord and his anointed king (132). The Lord made promises to David – 'my faithful love promised to David' as Isaiah (55:3) called them,[2] and they will be kept – indeed, kept in the city the Lord chose, and to which he gave visible expression in the symbol of the 'ark of his might' (132:8, 13). Secondly (133), there is the sweet unity of the Lord's people, the brothers and sisters in his family, bringing 'for evermore' the blessing of 'life' (133:3). And, finally, those who once groaned in their exile in the blackness of Kedar (120:5, p. 28 above), are now safe, under the comfortable darkness of the night sky, ascribing blessing to the Lord, and, in turn, receiving blessing back from him (134).

That's it! Home at last! The walls of his city are around us, his king is over us, his people are with us, his worship preoccupies us, his blessing enriches us, the blanket of the night sky of the Lord who made heaven and earth quiets our hearts in worship, wonder, love and praise.

Come and live with me in heaven for a bit!

---

## Notes

1 By far the most interesting – and indeed neglected – view is the one to be found in E. W. Bullinger, *The Chief Musician* (London, 1908), and *The Companion Bible* (OUP, undated); and in J. W. Thirtle, *The Titles of the Psalms* (London, 1904). They link the 'going up' with the 'stairway' (same word) of 2 Kings 20:11 and Isaiah 38:8, and ascribe the whole series to Hezekiah as he meditated on that 'sign'.

2 Compare Psalm 89:19–29.

## Psalm 132

## 17 The Lord in Zion: How he turns our plans upside down

David had a great idea,[1] and his prophet, Nathan, thought it a great idea too. It was a typical David plan: the Lord had taken him from shepherding his father's sheep, looked after him in all sorts of dodgy situations, and finally brought him to his throne and palace, with all its attendant luxuries. So was it not time for him to see the Lord equally well settled in a house?

### The tent and the house

You see, that was the way the Lord had brought his people up to think: he was mighty beyond all thought. Even the heaven of heavens could not contain him. Nevertheless, so that his people might really know that he was among them, he had directed that his tent be placed right at the very centre of their tents.[2] But now that they had left their camping, mobile-home days behind them, should not the Lord have his house at the centre of their houses?

It was a good plan, and the Lord liked it (1 Kings 8:18), but there were difficulties in the way. David was more than occupied with war

(1 Kings 5:3), and Moses had, as a matter of fact, foretold that the place of the Lord's dwelling must await the day when enemies were subdued on every side (Deuteronomy 12:10, 11). More than that, however, war and bloodshed had themselves unfitted David for building the Lord's house (1 Chronicles 22:7, 8), for, just think, how can a man of war build a house of peace? The great plan would, therefore, be implemented by one whose name would be Solomon, the man of peace, but, in the meantime, another building would be put in hand: the Lord would build David a house, a dynastic house, a line of kings for ever. Thus David's plan (2 Samuel 7:5) was turned on its head (2 Samuel 7:11); the costly work of the human king was turned upside down to become the work of divine grace – as it turned out, far more costly in the event, when great David's greater Son, the Son of God, baptized his kingliness in the blood of Calvary.

### The fact that became a song

2 Samuel 7:1–17, in this way, provided the pattern for Psalm 132, in which David's sworn promise to the Lord (verses 2–5) is transposed by grace into the Lord's sworn promise to David (verses 11–14). Who was it, we wonder, who meditated in this way on the episode in 2 Samuel 7, and composed this fine poem? When was it first sung? Maybe David wrote it himself in readiness for the day he brought the ark of the Lord to Zion (2 Samuel 6); maybe Solomon – or some other – wrote it to be used at the dedication of the temple (1 Kings 8);[3] maybe it was part of the temple-based 'reformation' of Josiah (2 Kings 22 – 23);[4] maybe Bullinger was right that Hezekiah wrote it;[5] maybe it was prompted by the building of the second temple in the days after the return from exile (Ezra 3:8–13) and in the later days of Haggai;[6] maybe we should go later still to the time of Nehemiah;[7] or maybe we just do not know, and it does not matter! In the Songs of the Great Ascent, it celebrates how the Lord gently sets aside the best and best-intentioned of human proposals, and replaces them with his own infinitely better purposes, resting on a more sure oath, and confirmed by far better promises. In this way, a song from the past becomes, to us, a voice for the present and a glory for the future.

## Getting the whole picture

Before getting to grips with some of the great truths of Psalm 132, please
– *please* – read and reread the whole psalm through, along the lines of
the following outline. Make its details familiar, and be clear about the
unity and structure of the whole.

** The psalm 'hangs' on three verses referring to David: verse 1 prays
that the Lord will credit to David's account all the trouble he has taken;
verse 10 asks that – again for David's sake – the Lord will favour his
anointed king; and, finally, in verses 17–18 the Lord responds that he
intends to establish a strong, anointed monarchy 'for David', victorious
and flourishing.[8]

** The first and second of these 'David' verses are followed by parallel
sections: verses 2–9 record David's oath to the Lord (verse 2) and its
consequences (verses 3–9), and verses 11–16 report how the Lord
'trumped' David's oath with his own oath to David (verse 11) and how
he intends to fulfil it (verses 11–16).

The psalm, then, looks like this:

A$^1$ (v. 1) Plea: Reward David for all the trouble he took
  B$^1$ David's oath to the Lord: Fact (2) and content (3–5)
    C$^1$ National participation (6–7)
      D$^1$ Prayer (8–9)
A$^2$ (v. 10) Plea: For David's sake, do not turn from the Anointed
      One
  B$^2$ The Lord's oath to David: Fact (11a) and content (11b–12)
    C$^2$ Divine ratification (13–14)
      D$^2$ Promise (15–16)
A$^3$ (vv. 17–18) Pledge: The guaranteed future of David's throne

## Payback time?

It sounds rather odd to our ears that anyone should pray, 'Right, Lord,
it's payback time!' Yet that is, is it not, what verse 1 says, in so many words?
'David went to a lot of trouble for you. What about remembering

him?' Yes, it does sound odd, even more plainly so when it is rendered literally: 'remember for David', that is to say, for his advantage or to his credit.

The thought, however, is not uncommon in the Bible, and, in fact, as we shall see, it is pretty important. Nehemiah offers the clearest example, actually ending his book with the plea 'Remember me with favour, O my God' (Nehemiah 13:31). He had just been busy purging the people of sinful ways and seeking to establish the priests and Levites in their religious duties – even down to the detail of making sure there was a wood supply for the altar. Then the plea – 'Lord, don't forget to credit me with all this!'[9] Even more importantly, there is a clear New Testament equivalent. Hebrews (6:10) says that God is not unjust, and consequently will not forget your work and the way you have loved him and helped his people. Paul wrote to the Thessalonians (2 Thessalonians 1:6–7) of how the justice of God makes certain that there will be 'payback time' – trouble to those who trouble you and relief to you who are troubled. More dramatically (1 Corinthians 3:12–15), he pictures each of us as building on the sole foundation of Jesus. It is a matter of enormous importance whether we are building in gold, silver, precious stones, wood, hay or straw, seeing that our work will be tested by fire. What survives the fire will receive its reward. 'Reward' – that's the thing, to secure our reward. Or, in 1 Corinthians 9:24, using another picture, he counsels us to race as those determined to win, or, in Philippians 3:14, to join him in focusing on the winning line so as to gain the prize. As Paul makes it so very clear in 1 Corinthians 3:15, this is not a salvation issue. We are not called to all this painstaking effort, this determination to build in gold, this ambition to be winners, in order that we may earn salvation, but because we have been saved. It matters to God how his children live, and the rewards of grace await those who commit themselves to the obedient life of grace. Therefore Paul prayed for his Colossians that they would 'live a life worthy of the Lord, and . . . please him in every way: bearing fruit in every good work, growing in the knowledge of God' (1:10). In the same spirit, he wrote to the Philippians that, while he deeply appreciated their generosity to him, his deeper longing was 'for what may be credited to your account' (4:17). One final example – and the highest of all: the Lord Jesus Christ, in his Sermon on the Mount, sets out, in Matthew 6:1–18, the motivating principle behind the life he wants his disciples to live – their 'acts of righteousness' (6:1). Every area of life – charity (to others), 2–4, prayer (to God), 5–15, and discipline (towards the self), 16–18 – must shun ostentation and the desire for human praise, and, on the contrary, be lived only for the eye of the heavenly Father – and for his reward.

Maybe we would not – of course we would not – nudge our heavenly Father: 'Did you see that? Have you spotted that? You'll mark it down for a reward, won't you?' – but the Old Testament, we find, frequently has its own blunt way of putting a truth, and so it is that, here in Psalm 132:1, the Lord is reminded, so to speak, to keep his ledgers up to date, with every detail recorded. David had indeed 'accepted trouble and humiliation'[10] – his times of danger at Saul's court, his years as an outlaw, a cave-dweller and an exile, all patiently endured as he, believingly, waited for the promise of kingship to be fulfilled, all lived under the self-restraining discipline, so faithfully discharged, of loyalty to Saul, the 'Lord's Anointed', who was anything but loyal to him. And, after he acceded to the throne, he forewent the pleasures and privileges of home (verse 3a), marriage (verse 3b), and sleep (verse 4) in his concern for the ark. Quite an example to us, we can certainly say, of going all out for the reward, of living for the Lord's pleasure and not our own. 'Put it all to David's account, Lord.'

### David, the covenant head

Please see with me how important it is that we should deliberately set ourselves to live so as to please our heavenly Father. We might hesitate to call on him to reward us (though the Old Testament does not); indeed, we might be a shade suspicious about giving too much prominence to the whole idea of reward (though the New Testament is not), but the fact remains that, moved by the Lord's saving mercies, our objective is to live the transformed life, devoting ourselves to what is good, well pleasing (to him) and perfect, namely, the will of God (Romans 12:1–2). So let's get on with it!

But, important as it is for us, it was much more so for David, as so much more depended on him. By the choice and anointing of God (1 Samuel 16:11–13), David became head man in the divine covenant. Just as Noah was covenant head in the Lord's rescue plans for the whole world,[11] and Abraham was covenant head in the Lord's purpose to restore to all nations the blessedness they needed and had lost,[12] so, when God's covenant of grace was given its royal development, David became its anointed head, the promise-bearer of what came to be called (NKJV) 'the sure mercies of David' (Isaiah 55:3), and the one through whom alone the promises would come to their fulfilment. Psalm 89:19–29 sets out the two promises that were covenanted to David, namely that, as the Lord's anointed (verses 19–23), he would yet reign over the whole created order (verses 24–27), and that his throne would be everlasting (verses 28–29).[13]

These promises are, of course, sovereign statements of divine intent. Nevertheless, just as, within the covenant with Abraham, Abraham's own life and conduct mattered,[14] so, as the sequence of events in Psalm 132 shows, it was when David made his spiritual commitment (verses 2–4) that the joyful participation of his people followed (verses 5–9); and, furthermore, it was consequent upon David's oath (verse 2) that the greater oath of the Lord followed (verse 11a), pledging the endless rule (verses 11b–12), the blessedness of Zion, divinely chosen and indwelt (verses 13–16), and, by implication, in promising the defeat of enemies (verses 17–18), David's universal sway.

## Godly king, godly people: The heart of true religion (verses 6–9)

2 Samuel 6:5, in its sober way, records how (literally), 'all the people' joined David in bringing up the ark. 1 Chronicles 13:2–8 goes into greater detail about the national joy of the occasion, with celebration, songs, harps, lyres, tambourines, cymbals and trumpets. A veritable 'Festival of Israel'! In a mere seven words the Hebrew of verse 6 captures the whole spirit of exuberance that was felt nationally.[15] The picture is reminiscent of the children's game 'hunt the thimble', as popular enthusiasm determined to run the ark to earth, following up rumours from the distant past.[16]

There was, however, more to the search than a national holiday. The enthusiasm of the chase in verse 6 becomes the call to worship in verse 7! The ark is not prized as a mere religious artefact – some visible aid to worship – nor because it is 'loaded' with ancient tradition and is rich in symbolism. These are the false trails that turn religion into ritual, and spirituality into superstition. No, the ark is sought because it is the place where the heavenly God 'touches down' on earth, 'his footstool', the 'real presence' of the Lord at the centre of Israel's religion, the point where eternity entered time, where holiness came to live on earth, where needy sinners were assured of atonement, acceptance on the ground of the shed blood, where the holy God was propitiated by a substitutionary sacrifice, and God's voice spoke by way of revelation to his people.[17]

Here, then, are the first two elements of true religion. True religion is not enthusiasm for religious pursuits and objects (verse 6), but consists of our personal approach into the presence of the Lord (verse 7a), and our bowing low in worship before the living presence of the Holy God who is our Redeemer (verse 7b).

The third element of true religion comes in verse 8: prayer that the Lord will come home among his people, and make his presence real, in all his power as the Saviour of sinners. This is the only place in the Psalms where the ark is mentioned, and it is given the title 'the ark of your might', that is to say, 'the ark that defines what your power really is', or, as the old prayer put it, addressing the Lord as the One 'who declarest thine almighty power most chiefly by showing mercy and pity'.[18] Earthquake, wind and fire, and every other manifestation of creational force do, of course, show the power of the Lord, but, far and away beyond all that, here is the very essence of his power. The ark, on the one hand, housed the tablets of the law before which we are all judged, condemned, sentenced and banished from the Lord's presence. On the other hand, over the condemning law was placed what William Tyndale movingly called 'the mercy seat', (NIV, the 'atonement cover'), the place where the atoning blood was sprinkled on the Day of Atonement. This, then, is the heart and summit of the Lord's power,[19] the divine provision by which mercy triumphed over judgment, and by which the broken law, in all its ferocity of condemnation, was 'covered' by the shed blood of a substitutionary sacrifice. This is the power which, finally, would tear apart the veil of separation and open the way into the holiest place through the blood of Christ.[20]

Two further elements of true religion remain, and in verse 9 each is sought in prayer from the Lord: priests who are what they are meant to be, and people who exult in the Lord's love. Or, putting the matter another way, mediation through which we can come to God, and exultant confidence in his presence as his loved ones.

## The priesthood, the priests, and the Priest

The Old Testament teaches that we need a mediatorial priesthood by which to approach God. Think of it pictorially. Only the priests could carry the ark; we, non-priests, could not approach it. Only the priests could minister at the altar of God, offering our burnt offerings, sin offerings and fellowship offerings. Only the priests could enter tabernacle or temple to make the incense offering and trim the light. Only the high priest – and he only once a year – could enter the Holy of Holies, within the veil, and sprinkle the atoning blood.[21] Yet without these functions we, the Lord's people, have no standing before him, no drawing near to him. Here, then, is another picture: in Exodus 40:35 we read that 'Moses could not enter the Tent of Meeting because the cloud had settled upon it, and the glory of the Lord filled' it. But read on into the first two verses of Leviticus: 'The Lord called to Moses . . . from the Tent of Meeting . . . When any of you brings an offering . . . ' Both the verb 'brings' and the noun 'offering' are derived from the verb 'to come near'. In a word, where holiness excludes, the sacrifices bring near – but only (as Leviticus teaches) through the mediating ministry of the priesthood.

The relation of this truth to the New Testament is almost too obvious to need saying, but it nevertheless has to be stated with care – positively and negatively. Positively, the Lord Jesus Christ is the only priest we need, and in the New Testament he is the only one to whom the word 'priest' in the singular refers. He has offered the one sacrifice for sins for ever; he is the perfect priest for us; through him alone and through him only we come to God. Negatively, the New Testament knows nothing of an 'order' of 'priests' standing between the Lord's people and the Lord. Like the sacrifices, the Old Testament priesthood finds its fulfilment and conclusion in Jesus, just as the Lord's intention to have a 'kingdom of priests' (Exodus 19:6) finds its fulfilment in the 'priesthood of all believers'.

## His saints, his beloved ones

The final element in true religion comes in the second part of verse 9, and centres on the word translated 'saints'. Its meaning has been strangely disputed, and it has received many different translations, but, briefly, this is its story. It is an adjective from the noun 'steadfast love', and the issue to be decided is whether the adjective is active (those who love the Lord) or passive (his beloved). The balance of evidence points to a passive meaning, the Lord's beloved ones, those who have been brought within the embrace of his love.[22] The intention of verse 9b, therefore, is that, matching the priesthood they need, the Lord's people come together, not primarily to express their love for him, but to revel in his love for them.

## The Davidic future

Psalm 132 begins (verse 1) with David's past and the rewards due to him; at its centre (verse 10) it seeks present mercies 'for the sake of your servant David', for in choosing him as covenant head, the Lord made lasting promises, 'the sure mercies of David'; the psalm ends (verses 17–18) by looking forward to secure blessing yet to come, 'for David'.

There are three chief blessings to be fulfilled. First, there is the city yet to be (verses 13–16), in which all that was implicit in the old Jerusalem (verse 7–9) will be fully realized: the city where the Lord resides (verses 13–14), where needs are fully met (verse 15), where there is a true priesthood and a rejoicing people (verse 16).

Secondly, there is priesthood in its full perfection. It might, at first sight, seem to be odd that Exodus tells us about the priestly robes (chapter 28) before it speaks of priestly people, Aaron and his sons (chapter 29). But this is deliberate. The garments reveal what the priest is meant to be. His closest-fitting undergarments were of pure linen (28:42), for the priest was to be a person of total inner purity; his most striking outer wear was the medallion of pure gold on his forehead, proclaiming his 'Holiness to the Lord' (28:36–37). In the light of this, poor old Aaron didn't have a chance! His first need (29:4) was washing, and, after that, a sin offering (verses 10–14). In other words, he wore the clothes that proclaimed what a priest should (and must) be, but he was not and could not be himself that priest. In the old Jerusalem they prayed for priests 'clothed with righteousness'. Since they were hardly praying for the provision of the right garments, this must be a prayer for priests as fully and perfectly righteous as their clothing professed. In response the Lord promises, in the Jerusalem yet to be, priests ministering salvation (verse 16), effective in their saving ministry to the sinners who, through them, draw near to God.

In the ultimate fulfilment, it will turn out that the plural 'priests' was always intended as a plural of majesty, for we 'have a great high priest' ministering grace (Hebrews 4:14–16); 'Such a high priest meets our need – . . . holy, blameless, pure, set apart from sinners' (Hebrews 7:26); 'this priest' who 'offered for all time one sacrifice for sins' and 'sat down at the right hand of God' awaiting the submission of every foe (Hebrews 10:12–13).

## 'Great David's greater son'[23]

David's 'horn' (his personal, conquering power) will yet truly (literally) 'sprout' (verse 17a);[24] the Lord's 'anointed'[25] will be as a lamp trimmed by the Lord himself; enemies will wear the clothes that proclaim their defeat and failure, and the disappointment of all they set out to achieve;[26] and the coming king will wear a crown proclaiming his own holy consecration.[27] What a king! What a prospect! But the reality has far outstripped even this forecast!

> In Thee, most perfectly expressed,
> The Father's glories shine:
> Of the full Deity possessed,
> Eternally Divine:
> Worthy, O Lamb of God, art Thou,
> That every knee to Thee should bow.[28]

---

## Notes

1  2 Samuel 7:1–3.
2  Exodus 29:42–46. Think of the 'layout' in Numbers 2 as cruciform, with the tribal camps in line east, south, west and north, and the Lord's tent at the crossing.
3  F. D. Kidner takes 2 Chronicles 6:41, 42 as a quotation from the psalm, which, therefore, must have existed in time for the dedication of the temple. See his volumes on Psalms in the Tyndale Old Testament Commentary series (IVP, 1973, 1975).

4 The prayer for the Lord's 'anointed' (verse 10) could well suggest that the monarchy was still in operation.

5 Bullinger, *The Chief Musician*, pp. 248–249, 308–311.

6 Ezra 4:24 – 5:1; 6:14, 15; Haggai 1:13–14.

7 See Wilcock, Vol. 2, p. 242.

8 Since the NIV does not offer the required translation 'for David' (*l'dawid*) in verse 1 it fails to show how this forms an 'inclusio' or bracket with *l'dawid*, 'for David', in verse 17. The NKJV does not have 'for David' in either verse! The ESV reads 'in David's favour' in verse 1 and 'for David' in verse 17. Even the RV slips up on this important parallel.

9 Compare Nehemiah 5:19; 13:14, 22, 31. In each case the original wording is, as in Psalm 132:1, 'remember for me', i.e. as something to my advantage or credit.

10 The verb √*anah* means 'to be low'. 'The hardships he endured' is the intensive passive participle (*pual*), translated 'afflicted' in Psalm 119:71; Isaiah 53:4, and in Leviticus 23:29 'deny himself', of a person imposing on himself the disciplines of the Day of Atonement. This last reference best illustrates Psalm 132:1: David 'accepted the humiliations and endured the trials'.

11 Genesis 9:11.

12 Genesis 12:1–3.

13 On Isaiah 55:3 and Psalm 89, see Alec Motyer, *The Prophecy of Isaiah* (IVP, 1993), p. 453; *Isaiah*, Tyndale Old Testament Commentaries (IVP, 1999), p. 344.

14 Genesis 12:1: the call to obedience preceded the statement of promise (verses 2–3); 18:17–19; 22:15–18.

15 See 1 Samuel 6:21 – 7:1 for the deposition of the ark in Kiriath Jearim. Taking into account the time mentioned in 1 Samuel 7:2; the passing years until Samuel's old age and the request for a king (1 Samuel 8:1), Saul's forty years (Acts 13:21) and David's seven years as king in Hebron (2 Samuel 2:11), at the time David resolved to restore the ark it could have been 100 years since its 'disappearance' from the scene, and it could well have involved a hunt to locate it.

16 1 Chronicles 13:5 identifies 'the fields of Jaar/the wood' with Kiriath Jearim ('the city of the woods'); compare 1 Samuel 6:21ff. 'Ephrath/ah' is a personal name (1 Chronicles 2:19, connected with Kiriath Jearim); a place name, identified with Bethlehem (Genesis 48:7; compare Ruth 4:11: Micah 5:2) – the area in which Bethlehem was situated? It also

seems to describe a class of person (Ruth 1:2; 1 Kings 11:26). See
1 Samuel 1:1 the Hebrew calls Elkanah 'an Ephrathite' which NIV
represents by 'Ephraimite'. In the psalm, it looks like the area within
which rumour placed the ark, which was finally tracked down to 'the
fields of Jaar'.

17 Leviticus 16:11–17. In Leviticus 16:20–22, the visible ceremony of the goat
was intended to display to the watching people the meaning of what
they were not permitted to see when the high priest alone entered the
Holy of Holies: a sin-bearing substitute, a total and final bearing of sin.
On the ark, see also Exodus 29:42–46.

18 The *Book of Common Prayer*, Collect for the Eleventh Sunday after
Trinity.

19 The first half of Psalm 132 emphasizes the awesomeness of divine
power. Twice the Lord is 'the Mighty One of Jacob' (verses 2, 5) –
'mighty' is *'abiyr*, sheer power. In verse 8 the more 'ordinary' word *'oz* is
used, to show how this terrifying power is focused on the ark, with all
its saving significance.

20 Exodus 26:31–34; Leviticus 16:11–17; Mark 15:37, 38; Hebrews 9:11–15, 24;
10:11–14, 19–23.

21 See Numbers 4:15; Joshua 6:12; Leviticus 1:5; Hebrews 10:11; Exodus
30:7–8; 2 Chronicles 26:16–21; Leviticus 16:2–3; Hebrews 9:7.

22 The noun is *chesedh*, the covenanted love of the Lord, his unchanging,
unconditional commitment to love his people. The adjective takes the
form *chasiydh*, sharing this formation with eighty-eight Hebrew words,
of which sixty-six clearly require a passive meaning; most of the
remaining twenty-two cannot be made to bear on the debate, and a
very few are plainly active (e.g. *'ariyts*, 'striking terror'). Occasionally
*chasidh*, like *chesedh*, is extended to express the covenanted love that
should obtain between individuals within the covenant, and
occasionally it expresses the faithful love we should return to the Lord.

23 Words from James Montgomery's hymn 'Hail to the Lord's anointed'.

24 √*tsamach*, 'to sprout, spring up' provided the messianic title 'the
Branch', e.g. Jeremiah 23:5; Zechariah 3:8; 6:12–13. 'Branch' is a 'family
tree' metaphor. The Messiah will descend from David. In its usage
'Branch' came to signify the Messiah as the King–Priest.

25 'anointed', *mashiach*, his Messiah. The 'lamp' recollected the perpetual
holy light in the tabernacle, trimmed (the same word as here) by the
high priest (Exodus 27:20–21). Did Aaron know that the lovely sevenfold

light was symbolic of the coming 'Light of the World', the Messiah, Jesus, Son of David, Son of God?

26  'Shame' is used more of disappointed hopes than of mere embarrassment – though including the latter.

27  The same word (*nezer*) is used of crown (Psalm 89:39), naziriteship (Numbers 6:7), and consecration (Leviticus 21:12, 'the consecration of the anointing oil', see NKJV).

28  J. Conder, 'Thou art the everlasting Word'.

Psalm 133

# 18 The family in Zion: The blessing of fellowship

Here is a gem of a psalm, beautiful in expression, clear in thought and structure, attractive in promise, practical and achievable in the vision it presents, and, above all, important – even challenging – in its truth. When we see its structure, we see it all:

| | | |
|---|---|---|
| v. 1 | Situation | |
| | | Fact: Brothers together |
| | | Experience: Brothers united |
| vv. 2–3a | Illustrations | |
| | | Festival anointing (on the head) |
| | | Holy anointing (Aaron) |
| | | Supernatural anointing (dew) |
| v. 3b | Explanation | |
| | | The place of blessing |
| | | The command to bless |
| | | The blessing that is commanded |

So, then, what is the psalm 'all about'? It is about the Lord's family ('brothers'), gathered, finding themselves in happy union with each other, and discovering that this is the situation the Lord delights to bless.

Psalm 133 conducts a wedding. The bridegroom is unitedness (verse 1), and the bride who comes to him in divine blessing is life (verse 3). These two are eternally bound together.

Follow the psalm through again. It opens (verse 1) with an exclamation: the goodness and delightfulness of the united family. Such a family meets with enrichment (verses 2–3a); the attentions of a welcoming host anointing each guest (Psalm 23:5). This is the 'oil of gladness' (Psalms 45:7; 104:15), but it is also much more than that, for it is the consecrating oil that Aaron knew (Exodus 29:7; Leviticus 8:12). Above all, it is supernatural, a down-running gift of God, his gentle and refreshing dew. And what is the explanation of all this glad richness? It is 'because' (verse 3, NIV 'for') they have come into a 'place' ('there'), a perpetuity ('for evermore'), and a certainty ('commanded')[1] of blessing, namely life.

### First: The place

'Blessing' is a broad word for the Lord's gracious response to our needs. When we pray – as we often must when we are ignorant of a friend's specific needs – 'Lord, please bless . . . ', we are, in fact, asking the Lord to review our friend's case and to react appropriately in meeting the needs he has seen. It is a loving and potent way to pray, for it brings our friends into the immediate presence of the Lord, and then leaves the outcome to him. There is, of course, no such thing as 'blessing' in isolation from the Lord himself. When he revealed the priestly formula of blessing in Numbers 6:23–27, he said first, 'This is how you are to bless the Israelites' (verse 23), and then he defined what actually happened as 'so they will put my name on the Israelites, and I will bless them' (verse 27). In other words, just as 'grace' is the Lord himself being gracious, himself coming to us in all his grace, so 'blessing' is the Lord drawing near to us in all his amplitude of sufficiency for every need. In 'blessing', he comes to share himself with us, here, in verse 3, bringing 'life'.

It makes little difference whether we attach the words 'for evermore' to the noun 'life' – i.e. he comes with the blessing of eternal life – or whether 'for evermore' defines the permanency of the command, or, as the NIV would have it, of the bestowal. Either way, the blessing is guaranteed, and its continuance is for ever. 'Life', says the psalm, is 'the blessing',[2] i.e. the blessing of all blessings, as indeed it must be, because 'life', too, is inseparable from the Lord: we can have divine life only when he comes to impart himself to us. Jesus said, 'I have come that they may have life, and have it to the full' (John 10:10), 'eternal life' (John 6:40), 'everlasting life' (John 6:47), the life that is ours by feeding on Jesus himself (John 6:57).

This unique blessing, this most covetable blessing, the indwelling presence of the Lord in all his vitality, can be had only 'there' (verse 3). Just as when Jesus said, 'Go to Galilee; *there* they will see me', meeting the risen Lord was conditional on travelling to the place of meeting, so we must ask, where is this 'place' where the life of God becomes ours?

### The 'place' of brotherly unity

Psalm 133 is entitled 'Of David', and, as with all the Davidic ascriptions, there is no reason to doubt authorship by the 'sweet psalmist of Israel' (2 Samuel 23:1, NKJV).[3] Was the psalm possibly prompted by the national unity enjoyed in Psalm 132:6–9 (2 Samuel 6:2)? Why not? For this sense of national cohesion was a mark of David's early reign, following the dislocations left by Saul. But for sure there is no problem in seeing the suitability of the psalm for the Book of Pilgrim Praise. Think of family groups setting out from some village, as Joseph and Mary set out with their family in later days (Luke 2:41). A few miles down the road similar groups join them from another village. They have not met since the same time last year. As the journey proceeds, the company grows larger as more and more travelling companies converge, all one in their common faith and their common destination, and soon to be part of a huge union and unity in Zion! How good! How very good indeed!

There is one thing that the psalm underlines, when translated literally. They are all 'brothers', siblings, male and female, belonging to the same family; but they are 'also together'. The journey is over; individual family units have merged into ever larger and larger companies until all are gathered – one great family assembly before the Lord. But they are *also* 'in unity'. Families as such are not always united; they are frequently at loggerheads, or in a state of armed neutrality. Churches

assemble, but, though in one place, may not be at one. Such together-
ness is something extra, something special, to be treasured when present,
to be sought when absent. This is what the psalm calls 'good', i.e.
objectively and in itself a good thing; but it is also 'delightful', the
source of pleasure, and, at best, of unutterable happiness, when ties of
membership and of assembly are also ties of heart and mind[4] – having
the same mind, as Paul would say (Romans 12:16), the same animation
and aim (Philippians 1:27), thinking the same thing and prompted by
the same love (Philippians 2:2–4). It is of no small importance to notice
that when Paul had written to the Ephesians about their divinely planned
and grace-based salvation (Ephesians 1:3–4; 2:4–8) and then turned to
delineate the life that should now follow, his first call is that we should
'keep the unity of the Spirit through the bond of peace' (4:3). The Bible,
and the Lord of the Bible, wants us to enjoy the good life and to revel
in it – but first to make it our aim.

## The great down-pouring

David would also say it is worth pursuing because it prompts a heavenly
response, a down-pouring of blessing. Three times he uses the verb
'running down'. Where 'brethren' are 'together' ' – *and* at one' – it is as
if 'precious oil' were 'running down' on the head; as if holy oil were
'running down' on Aaron; as if Hermon's dew were 'falling' on Zion.
Truly the floodgates of heaven have been opened (Malachi 3:10).

** The first picture is one of well-being. Oil, says Psalm 104:15, is God's
provision to make a person's face shine. It symbolizes transformation
from sorrow to joy (Isaiah 61:3). It is the act of a welcoming host to
enhance his guest's sense of welcome at the feast (Psalm 23:5). By
implication, oil speaks of the gift of the Holy Spirit (1 Samuel 16:13;
compare 2 Samuel 23:1–2).

** The second picture is of consecration. Oil has been used in some
abundance – for the gifts of God are never ungenerous – 'running down'
from head to beard, but this prompts a fresh development of the idea:
Aaron's beard, and the unique oil of priestly consecration (Exodus
30:22–33). It must surely rank as a supreme curiosity of interpretation

when David is understood to mean that Aaron's beard 'went down to the hem of his garment'! No, it is this same thought of the abundance of consecrating oil flowing over the head, through the beard and all round the wide collar of 'the robe of the ephod' (Exodus 28:31), a poncho-like outer garment for the priest. So Aaron was anointed (Exodus 29:7) and his anointing set him apart, 'sanctified him', for his holy functions (Leviticus 8:12). In this way he became a shadow cast before it by the great coming event of the One to whom the Lord God would give his Spirit without measure (John 3:34), our great high priest, Jesus, but Aaron was also a picture of each individual in the coming 'kingdom of priests' – in other words, the Lord has in hand a copious anointing for every individual in the priesthood of all believers, enduing, setting apart for holy living, equipping us by his Spirit to live out in daily life the actuality of the priesthood that is ours through the cross of Christ (Hebrews 10:19–25; Revelation 1:5–6).

** The third picture is of a supernatural miracle. This is the third 'coming down', the 'falling' of 'the dew of Hermon' on Mount Zion. 'Dew' is itself an image of the gentle ways of the Lord in blessing his people: his provision for fruitfulness (Genesis 27:28; Deuteronomy 33:13); his life-giving power to raise the dead (Isaiah 26:19);[5] his gift of life to his people (Hosea 14:5), and their gracious influence among the nations (Micah 5:7). All this can be taken into the promise of the psalm, but what about the 'dew of Hermon' falling on 'Mount Zion'? Start by recalling the north–south divide of the twelve tribes. Remember how, in the event, it seems to have been easy for Jeroboam to lead off the ten tribes of the north to form the separate kingdom of 'Israel' (1 Kings 12) – or, indeed, for Absalom even during David's kingship (2 Samuel 15:2–6). It is quite clear that there was already a long-standing fissure waiting to be exploited. It goes back even further. Saul bequeathed the same division to David, so that the 'Judah' tribes (2 Samuel 2:4) and the 'Israel' tribes (2 Samuel 5:1) came separately to invite David to accept kingship. It was the genius of David's leadership that brought the divided people together around his kingship, the new capital city of Jerusalem, and the freshly established religious centre provided by the ark. He gave poetic expression to this in his psalm. Hermon was the prominent mountain of the north, as Zion was of the south, and David sees them as no longer in tension but belonging so naturally together that it is as if the dew of

Hermon could come and fall on Zion! It would be a miracle, of course, but then when enemies are reconciled, when coldness becomes love, when aloofness becomes closeness, and uncaring becomes concern – these things are all miracles too! By and under the blessing of God – his gentle, heavenly down-pouring – Hermon and Zion are at one in a shared blessing.

## Where there is unity, there falls the blessing

How to enjoy heavenly enrichment of personal life, how to live as the Lord's priestly, consecrated, holy people . . . If we want the blessing, look to the unity! The blessing is heavenly and miraculous. Only the Lord can command it. According to his word, the blessing 'runs down' to a particular, stated place – the place where 'brethren' come together – 'and in unity'. We should pray for it, cultivate it and practise it, and refuse to do, say or be anything that threatens it – and, of course, its first and primary focus is the local church to which you and I belong.

---

### Notes

1  So, literally, the verb √*tsawah* cannot mean anything else. Where did the NIV get 'bestows' from?

2  So, literally, 'because there the Lord commanded the blessing . . . ' It is, of course, 'his' blessing, but the psalmist intended rather to teach that this is the paramount blessing, blessing par excellence.

3  In verses 2b–3a we find a prefixed form of relative pronoun (*sh-*) attached to the participle 'running down', and some insist that this is an indication of late Hebrew. See, however, G. A. Cooke, *A Critical and Exegetical Commentary on Judges* (T. & T. Clark, 1908): 'The relative sh is frequent in late biblical Hebrew . . . but it is unsafe to infer that it was of late origin . . . ' (p. 144). It occurs, for example, in Judges 5:7, in a song that many attribute to Deborah herself, 'the oldest extant monument of Hebrew literature' (p. 132). Cooke is not known for conservative judgments. The relative *sh* may be derived from Aramaic, which 'often indicates an early not a late date' (New Bible Dictionary, under Arameans). Kitchen (*Ancient Orient and Old Testament* [Tyndale, 1966], p. 145) notes Aramaic penetration of Syria and Mesopotamia at the time of David.

4 The two words, 'good' and 'pleasant', respectively *tob* and *na'im*, offer no obvious distinction in their general use, but when together, as here, the former may be taken as the objective reality of something 'good', and the latter the subjective enjoyment and appreciation of it.

5 See Motyer, *Prophecy of Isaiah*, pp. 218–220; *Isaiah: An Introduction and Commentary*, TOTC, (IVP, 1999), pp. 177, 178.

Psalm 134

# 19 Worship in Zion: Safely home, richly blessed

My aunts – dear, pious ladies – always spoke of dying as being 'called to higher service'. I am not sure quite what they would make of Psalm 134. It addresses the 'servants' of the Lord, but, 'behold' (verse 1),[1] these servants are not engaged in any work, they are not busy, they are actually standing still (verse 1b); the whole 'feeling' of the scene is of calm and rest, the only movement is the raising of their hands. Yet, yes indeed, they are called to 'higher service', and are, in fact, engaged in it. This is a key truth to learn from the last of the Songs of the Great Ascent.

**'They also serve, who only stand . . . '**

The psalm brings us in to share night prayers in the temple, and breathes the quietness, peace and 'space' of all true night-time worship. It does not itself provide an answer to the question of who is calling whom to worship in verse 1, or who dismisses whom with blessing in verse 3. Some think of a kindly liturgy conducted between the daytime priests going off duty and the night-time priests coming on duty, but, since every such suggestion is only a theory, let us do our own theorizing, and keep Psalm 134 in the setting of the Songs of the Great Ascent, where it now belongs.

We pilgrims have at last reached the city of our dreams (122:2), and the instant cry of the younger members of our party, some maybe on their first visit, is 'Can we go and see the temple?' 'Oh', reply the fathers in their unimaginative way, 'It's far too late. You're far too tired. You need your beds.' But the youngsters won't be silenced. Besides, they know how to handle this situation. 'Mum, can we go and see the temple?' 'Why not?' say the more understanding mothers. 'Of course they want to see the temple – besides, we'll be just in time for night prayers.'[2] And so, under the canopy of the night sky, and with the silence of the slumbering city all around, the temple court is a very haven of peace and rest, and we enter[3] in time to hear the call to worship: 'Behold! Bless Yahweh, all you servants of Yahweh!'[4]

This is the end and goal of pilgrimage. The children were right! We set out on pilgrimage from our far country (Psalm 120), the Lord marvellously sheltered us on the way (Psalms 121, 124), we 'have come to Mount Zion' (Hebrews 12:22), and this is what we have come for: to stand in the Lord's presence, and to lift our hands in worship, and to receive his blessing. Not a climax of activity, of doing and striving and organizing and arduous endeavour, but the bowed head and the uplifted hand of adoration, worship, wonder, love and praise, where no voice is heard but that which cries aloud, 'Salvation belongs to our God who sits on the throne, and to the Lamb' (Revelation 7:10).

### Blessing and being blessed

It is hardly surprising that the NIV hesitated to translate the verb as 'bless' – indeed it is a matter for gratitude that other translations did not lose their nerve in the same way. For surely the question must be asked, how can we 'bless the Lord'? Obviously 'praise' is a general-purpose verb, but 'bless' cannot avoid being more specific in what it implies. Most likely the primary meaning of the verb (√barach) is 'to kneel down', which provides the noun (berech) a 'knee'.[5] In religious use, therefore, it is nearer 'to bow in worship' (132:7) than it is to 'praise'. The real clue, however, to what it means to 'bless the Lord' comes from noting that the same verb is used when he blesses us. What, then, does the expression 'May the Lord bless you' (verse 3) mean? It is a request for the Lord to look on us, discern our needs and meet them, that is to say, to review us and to respond. Likewise, when we bless the Lord, we – say it reverently – review him and respond. He reviews our needs; we review his revealed excellencies. 'To bless God', says F. D. Kidner, 'is to acknowledge gratefully what he is'. Blessing us, he would make us, by his sufficiency, what we are not; in blessing him, we bow low to acknowledge and revere what he is. To bless the Lord, therefore, is to call to mind the glorious things that he has revealed about himself, as well as the glorious things he has done, and to bring ourselves low, to kneel, in worship and adoration. This is the climax of pilgrimage. An elderly friend once said, 'I can't think why the Lord has taken Hilda and left me. He must have something left for me to do.' 'No,' responded another, 'He has nothing left for you to do but to go on loving him.' To wear for all eternity the blood-washed robes of white, to stand before the throne and sing of a salvation that is all of God; to pass gratefully into the shepherd-care of the Lamb – for who would know shepherding better than a lamb? – and to rejoice in his tear-free gift of life (Revelation 7:9–17).

Such worship does not, of course, need to wait till we reach our eternal home. It is the goal of pilgrimage for every day, as the word of God privately ministers to us its ever-deepening treasures of the revelation of God. It is the ideal to strive after when we join our fellow pilgrims in public worship on the Lord's day. For we are pilgrims in that strange but true situation of having already arrived at the city (Hebrews 12:22) to which we are also making our way (Revelation 21:9 – 22:5). As it will be then, so let it be now!

### Holy people, holy place

Very likely the too-frequently missing ingredient in our pilgrim worship is a properly awesome sense of God's presence. With the completion of the written word of God, he revealed himself to us richly, far more richly, indeed, than to our pilgrim relatives in the Old Testament, yet how deeply they sensed his presence; how sensitively and wholeheartedly they worshipped! They stepped through the gates of Jerusalem saying to themselves, 'This is the city the Lord chose for his actual dwelling place';

they entered the temple courts and looked at the sanctuary itself, saying, 'Here is his footstool' (132:7). They built the temple by command so that the Lord might come to them; we have our church buildings so that we might come to him. Oh, yes, we worship him in Spirit and truth, but they worshipped also in a wondrous consciousness of his real, near, and actual presence. We know that he is present where two or three are gathered in his name (Matthew 18:20), but do we come too casually? Do we pray sufficiently that the Lord will make his presence felt? Do we spend time preparing our hearts to 'bless the Lord'?

The psalm commands worshippers to 'lift up their hands in (or towards) the sanctuary (or, in holiness)' (verse 2). Uplifted hands were a common adjunct to worship,[6] here raised 'towards' the Holy of Holies where the Lord was present in all his holiness among his people. The word 'sanctuary' in the Old Testament does not have the meaning 'a place of safety', the sense in which we use it now, but always 'a place of holiness',[7] and, very frequently, the simple noun 'holiness' is used.[8] The tendency nowadays is to favour 'sanctuary' over 'holiness' in contexts such as Psalm 134, but, for example, 'holiness' is to be preferred to 'sanctuary' in Psalm 150:1. Why, however, should we not preserve all possible meanings? In worship we come to the very presence of God; we lift up our hands to acknowledge his presence and to direct our worship to him; we 'lift up holy hands', for stained hands are unacceptable,[9] and the blood of Jesus is our only means of entrance within the veil (Hebrews 10:19–22). Viewed in this fullness of meaning – 'holiness/holy place' – the word holds together our God-given status as his holy people, 'holy through the sacrifice of the body of Jesus Christ once for all' (Hebrews 10:10), and our God-given privilege of access. Our pilgrim partners of old could only look at the sanctuary and raise their hands in worship towards it, but 'we have confidence to enter the Most Holy Place by the blood of Jesus' (Hebrews 10:19).

### The God of Zion, the Maker of heaven and earth

With what reluctance, having reached the goal of our pilgrimage, and savoured the presence of the Lord God, and worshipped him, we would then turn from the courts of the Lord (Psalm 84:1–2, 10) to the dark streets of the city to make our way to our pilgrim lodgings! But what we are leaving behind we are also taking with us, a Zion blessing guaranteed by the power and all-sufficiency of the Maker of heaven and earth. For, as we have seen, 'blessing' is not something apart from the Lord's person. The blessing puts his name on us – that is, all that the Lord has revealed himself to be.

First, then, as 'Maker of heaven and earth', he is present in every place, sovereignly in control of everything, alongside us where we are, and in full possession of all the riches in glory that heaven contains, sufficient for every need. Secondly, since the blessing comes 'from Zion', it is centrally the blessing associated with the house of the Lord and the ark of the covenant, the blessing of atonement, reconciliation and sins once and for all forgiven, the blessing of a God to whom we come near through his appointed sacrifice, and whose love is pledged as a constant, unchanging reality.

----

## Notes

1 Omitted in the NIV. Why? It is an important word used by the inspiring Holy Spirit to call attention to something he wants us to be sure not to miss.

2 If our pilgrims were in Jerusalem for Passover, it was a night festival. Isaiah 30:29 maybe refers to Passover, but at any rate records night-time processions. 1 Chronicles 9:33 mentions musicians responsible for night duty, compare 23:30.

3 It is true that the verb 'to stand' is used of the priests and Levites on duty (e.g. Deuteronomy 18:5), but it is also used of the assembled congregation (Jeremiah 7:10; 28:5). It refers to the arriving pilgrims in 122:2; 135:2 addresses 'all who stand' (NIV, 'minister'), a general description of all the classes addressed in 135:19–21. Allen points out that the noun 'servants' is not used of priests or Levites, though the verb 'to serve' and the noun 'service' are.

4 On 'Behold', see chapter 18, note 2. In 134:1 it calls the congregation to attention as the evening worship is about to start. 'Bless' should not be reduced to 'praise', any more than, say, 'give thanks' should be rendered 'praise'. The verb 'to bless' (√*barach*) occurs here in verses 1–2 of 'blessing the Lord' and in verse 3 of his blessing us. It is the keyword of the psalm. See NKJV, RV, ESV, NASB and NRSV.

5  Brown, Driver and Briggs, *Hebrew and English Lexicon of the Old Testament* (Oxford, 1906), pp. 138–139; J. N. Oswald in *Theological Wordbook of the Old Testament* (Moody, 1980), Vol. 1, p. 132. Compare 1 Kings 8:54; 2 Chronicles 6:13.

6  E.g. Psalm 28:2; 1 Timothy 2:8.

7  Hebrew, *miqdash*.

8  *Qodesh*.

9  Isaiah 1:15; Psalm 24:4; James 4:8.

# Psalms 135 and 136
# 20 Singing the songs of homeland[1]

Psalm 135:2 makes a link back to 134:1, a link that is worth taking seriously. In Psalm 134 our pilgrims at last reached their goal, and took their stand not only within the gates of the city (122:2) but in the actual temple precincts. Was Psalm 135 part of their night-time worship, or was it, by custom, the opening hymn of worship on their first full day? We know nothing of these things and cannot give an answer. But it makes a great deal of sense to link Psalms 135 and 134 in this way, and, of course, Psalm 136 has so much in common with 135 that it demands to be part of the paean of praise that must surely have risen from every pilgrim heart.

## The great God of pilgrims

What better way for pilgrims to mark their safe arrival in Zion than by recalling the great foundational pilgrimage of Israel out of Egypt, 'through many dangers, toils and snares',[2] into the land of promise? And did it not stand to reason that when they too had ventured out on pilgrimage they would find themselves cared for in every circumstance and vicissitude, and safely gathered into Zion? If they were not thinking along these lines, they should have been, because the songs they were singing were, at heart, a reminder that the Lord their God first creates pilgrims, then guards them and supplies their needs, and finally brings them safely home into his city and house.

In any case, these were the truths that they were singing, for the heart of both psalms, 135 and 136, traces the great pilgrimage of the redeemed from Egypt to Canaan (135:8–14; 136:10–22). The accounts are identical in some of their details, and complementary in others, and together provide a compendium of truth about the Lord and his pilgrims.

### By redemption the Lord creates pilgrims

Each account of the great pilgrimage begins in Egypt, but, more importantly, at the same point in Israel's Egyptian experience. The verb 'struck down' (135:8; 136:10) recalls the power of the Lord over all the power of the enemy – and we need to bear constantly in mind that Egypt was then what would be called a superpower today. This is a truth to which the accounts will return, but the point that both accounts make is not the exercise of overmastering power but the exercise of power in judgment: the death of Egypt's firstborn. In short, pilgrimage began not with the departure from Egypt as such but on Passover night when the Lord passed through the land of Egypt, carrying out judgment on all the gods of Egypt, and exacting a terrible, even if only token, judgment on Pharaoh and his people for their persistent rejection of his word. All the firstborn in the land of Egypt died[3] while Israel, the Lord's firstborn (Exodus 4:22), was safe beneath the blood of the Passover lamb.[4] In addition, inside the blood-marked houses they were feasting on the lamb, already dressed for a journey. Passover was an evening meal, but it was eaten by people not in dressing gowns and slippers but with their cloaks tucked into their belts, shoes on their feet and staff in hand (Exodus 12:11), all ready for a journey! The Passover created pilgrims. Three things came together inseparably that night: the blood, the feast and the clothing. To be a pilgrim is part of the definition of being redeemed; to go on pilgrimage is not a second decision following that of accepting redemption through the blood of the lamb; it is of the essence of being redeemed.

### The Lord's pilgrims are given a complete redemption

While 135:10 moves directly from leaving Egypt to entering Canaan, 136:13–15 pause to recall how the Lord 'cut the Red Sea in two', and swept Pharaoh away.[5] At the time it must have seemed baffling to Israel that, by following the detailed map references given to Moses by the Lord (Exodus 14:2), they found themselves trapped between the advancing Egyptians and the barrier of the sea (Exodus 14:9). Obedience had certainly landed them in the soup! And if we feel inclined to criticize their panic-stricken cry (14:10) we are sadly lacking in self-knowledge. It was precisely the sort of situation that prompts the question 'Why?' But, like all situations that tempt us to say a disbelieving 'Why?', it was full of divine purposeful mercy. On the very occasion they panicked, and wondered what their redemption was all about (14:11–12), they were given the promise 'the Egyptians you see today you will never see again' (Exodus 14:13) and, right enough, they 'saw the Egyptians lying dead on the shore', and their unbelieving panic turned into glad recognition of 'the great power' of the Lord (Exodus 14:30–31). The Lord does not work redemption by halves. He promised to redeem (Exodus 6:6) and he so stage-managed his pilgrims' pathway that they experienced a finished work of redemption.[6]

### The Lord is sufficient for the needs of the pilgrim pathway

We are indebted again to Psalm 136:16 for the recollection of the journey through the wilderness. Deuteronomy 8:2–4 comments on this. It says that the journey humbled and tested the people – kept them humble by the constant realization that they were facing circumstances and hazards far beyond their natural ability to overcome; subjected them to testing whether they would rise to the occasion with the faith that resulted in obedience. But, throughout, the Lord faithfully fed them day by day, and maintained them in equipment and health. Taking events in turn, then, at the Red Sea, the Lord showed that he is sufficient to deal with barriers and hindrances to pilgrimage, circumstantial roadblocks; in the wilderness, he revealed that he is sufficient to cater for our personal needs; and, looking forward, both psalms record the victories over great and mighty kings in order to bring his pilgrims into the land he promised (135:10–12; 136:17–22) – he is sufficient against all hindrances and needs of the journey, and all the power of the enemy. The Lord is that one much stronger than the strong who binds the strong man and plunders his goods (Matthew 12:29).

### The Lord is revealed as the guardian of pilgrims

Psalm 135:8–14 is all the more impressive for being brief. There are three truths in sequence, like three great drumbeats:

** out of Egypt (verses 8–9),
** into Canaan (verses 10–12),
** an unchanging revelation of who the Lord is and what he does – and why (verses 13–14).

The last two verses here draw out the lesson of the previous five. The Lord's 'Name' is the summary, shorthand statement of what he wants us to know about himself. To Moses he revealed the meaning of his name, 'Yahweh' (Exodus 3:13–17), the ever-present and active One, and in particular the God present and active in the exodus events, the God who overthrows his enemies and redeems his people. But, says Exodus 3:15, this is his name for ever, and Psalm 135:13 reaffirms that what the Lord did and was for his exodus pilgrims remains everlastingly true. He is always the Lord who overthrows his enemies and saves his people,[7] because, says 135:14, the Lord will vindicate his people and have compassion on his servants – a pledge of abiding commitment. 'Vindicate' is the verb *diyn*, which is used here as if the Lord were an advocate at law taking on our case, and not for a fee, but truly *pro bono publico*, simply because of his unchanging compassion and care.[8]

### An absolute guarantee

These four great truths about pilgrims, their pilgrimage and their Lord come to us in Psalms 135 – 136 backed by a rock-solid guarantee. The structure of the psalms makes this clear:

| 135 | 136 |
|---|---|
| vv. 5–7 | vv. 4–9 |
| The ruler of creation | The Lord's wonders in creation |
| vv. 8–14 | vv. 10–22 |

The great pilgrimage: Egypt to Canaan
Redemption creates pilgrims; redemption is total
The Lord is sufficient; his guardian care is assured

| vv. 15–18 | vv. 23–25 |
|---|---|
| No other gods: dead idols, dead idolaters | The love that remembers, rescues and provides |

The message of this structure hardly needs to be amplified. Both psalms share the facts of the great pilgrimage, the exodus, and the truths about the pilgrims' Lord that undergird these facts. Psalm 135 brackets this by pointing on the one hand to the power of the Creator and on the other hand to the deadness of idol gods, and to their only capacity, the capacity to share their deadness with their adherents. How secure, then, are the Lord's pilgrims! They walk in his world, which, everywhere, is the sphere of his sovereign power; they are opposed only by the dead!

Where 135:6 calls attention to the Lord's unfettered power, in all creation, to do what he wills, 136:4 speaks of his 'great wonders', especially his wonders in ordering the creation according to his will. This truth is matched by reference not to dead idols, but (verses 23–25) to the perpetuity of the love that 'remembered' those at the bottom of life's heap, rescued and, with equally perpetual love, sustains. The wonders of creation are matched by the wonders of grace.

Truths typical of the Old Testament – therefore basic to the Bible – cluster in these verses.

First, look at the world around us and see the hand of God. It is not that the Bible ignores 'second causes', but rather that it is determined that we should always keep our eyes on the First Cause. Doubtless geographers have their own story to tell about vaporization and rainfall, about lightning and wind (135:7), about tectonic plates and the movement and luminosity of heavenly bodies (136:6–9), but to fail to look through, beyond and past such stories is like sitting at a signpost and imagining we have reached the destination! No, no! Go where the signs point! Look at the world around and see the hand of God. Do rainclouds gather? He has done it. Does wind blow? The winds and the waves obey him (Mark 4:41). Sentiment dwells on creation in its beauty, and this is right:

> The kiss of the sun for pardon,
> The song of the birds for mirth.
> One is nearer God's heart in a garden
> Than anywhere else on earth.

The realism of the Bible would agree, but also calls for stronger meat, for another verse to be added:

> The hiss of the rain for pardon,
> The howl of the wind for mirth.
> One is nearer God's heart in an earthquake
> Than anywhere else on earth.

Whether it is to be lifted up by beauty, awed by power or humbled by overwhelming force, God is there; he is great; he does what he wills in heaven and earth; 'the sea is *his*, for *he* made it, and *his* hands formed the dry land' (Psalm 95:5).

Secondly, there are no other gods. We need to remember that the people of the Old Testament – like the New – lived in a polytheistic world. When, therefore, the Bible seems to attribute 'existence' to other gods,[9] it is only raising a warning that the Lord's people are always faced with the challenge and the allure of alternative objects of worship. Such alternatives have no reality.[10] No doubt the thoughtful idolater saw his idol as a visible representation of an unseen, spiritual reality, but the Old Testament will have none of it. There is nothing behind or beyond the idol; it is a helpless, lifeless artefact – why, it has to be nailed in place or it will fall over (Isaiah 40:20).[11] Yet, grimly, the idol has one 'power' – to make its devotees like itself (Psalm 135:18).

But the whole point of the surrounding verses is this: to give the Lord's pilgrims his rock-solid guarantee. At every point on their pilgrimage they are in his world, where his writ runs; every experience of life is what his wisdom dictates; the forces ranged against them – whatever horrors they may be allowed to inflict (1 Corinthians 10:13) – are dead idols and their dead adherents. This is pilgrim security and assurance.


### 'Praise, my soul, the King of heaven'

If it is right to think of Psalms 135 – 136 as the songs the pilgrims sang when they reached their goal – and why not? – then their preoccupation was not with the journey they had made, but with the great salvation the Lord had achieved once for all when he redeemed his people by the blood of the Lamb. Thus the Old Testament bridges over into the New (as one would expect), and anticipates the innumerable company drawn from every nation, tribe, people and language, who, though each had come by an individual route out of 'great tribulation', sing with one voice 'Salvation belongs to our God, who sits on the throne, and to the Lamb' (Revelation 7:9–10). To God alone ascends the praise of his pilgrim people, gathered finally and eternally into his presence, and this is true also of the two psalms. They centre on the Lord's omnipotent and irresistible saving work, but they begin and end on the note of praise, blessing and thanksgiving.

** In Psalm 135:1–4 the divine Name is mentioned seven times,[12] four times the verb 'to praise' is used and once the verb (NIV 'sing praise') 'to make music'.

** In Psalm 135:19–21 the divine Name is mentioned seven times, four times the call goes out (verses 19–20) to 'bless' the Lord (NIV, 'praise'), once the call to praise (verse 20b) and once the Lord is pronounced 'blessed'.[13]

** In Psalm 136:1–3 the call is to give thanks, and this is taken up again in the last verse of the psalm. Thanksgiving dominates Psalm 136, being in principle reiterated by the repeated 'to him'. The threefold 'to him' in verses 4–9 is matched by the three acts of God in verses 23–25.

*Divine choice:* In Psalm 135:4 the reason given for praising the Lord is that 'he chose . . . Israel to be his treasured possession'. The historical verification of that choice was the redemption of Israel from Egypt, but, as Deuteronomy 7:6–8, reminds us, the root of the choice goes further back, and also deeper into the divine nature, for it is a product of love. To say that the Lord's love is 'unexplained' – all Moses can find to say, in effect, is that 'the Lord loves you because he loves you' – does not mean that it is arbitrary or intrinsically inexplicable. It simply means that the Lord has not chosen to reveal the reasons within his own nature that prompted his choice. It is his free choice; it is also sovereign, not to be questioned, never to be revoked. It is the abiding foundation of Israel: here in the psalm, later in Ephesians 1:3–4. Furthermore, having loved and chosen, the Lord remains delighted with what he has done: we are his 'treasured possession'. This great word, *sᵉgullah*, received its classical definition in Exodus 19:5. The Lord is the possessor of all, but, as is the case with all of us, within the totality of our possessions there is something we prize as specially ours, specially valued. So we are to the Lord. Peter says we are 'a chosen people . . . people belonging to God/(ESV) a people for his own possession'.[14] Every other blessedness follows from this; this is the ground of eternal praise to the God of our salvation.

*Unchanging salvation:* The pilgrims are safely home. Travelling days are done. The mobile home has been exchanged for the house not made with hands, eternal, in the heavens (2 Corinthians 5:1). Yet one thing remains unchanged: 135:21 (NKJV), 'Blessed be the Lord out of Zion, who dwells in Jerusalem.' Unto eternal days, Yahweh is still the holy God who meets his people and whose people draw near to him only on the grounds of the shed blood. The blood of the lamb – or, as we would now say, of the Lamb – is not only their passport (Revelation 21:27), but also their residence permit. Far be it from me to quibble with William Cowper. His words are too lovely to tamper with. He wrote:

> Dear dying Lamb, Thy precious blood
> Shall never lose its power
> Till all the ransomed church of God
> Are saved to sin no more.

'Till' has the sad implication of a terminus after which the blood of the Lamb is no longer needed. No, Cowper would not have meant that! But for as long as we sing his wonderful hymn[15] we need to say to ourselves, 'No, not even then! The blood of Jesus is my only security for all eternity.'

*Love 'ever-unchanging':* Twenty-six times Psalm 136 proclaims 'His love endures for ever'. This is the Lord's 'pledged love', not the love of 'falling in love' (he has that too!), but the love that listens to the wedding-day question 'Will you love her . . . ?' and answers 'I will'. The psalm traces everything back to that ever-unchanging love: out of it flows the Lord's goodness (verse 1), his wonders in the marvellous creation in which he has set us (verses 4–9), his redeeming work (verses 10–12), his power over our adverse circumstances (verse 13), and over the adversaries who would either undo our salvation (verses 15–17) or deprive us of our inheritance (verses 17–22). It is the reason for his concern for us, his